W9-AYQ-978

## *What Others Are Saying About In The SpotLight:*

Janet Esposito really demonstrates her expertise in the area of overcoming performance anxiety in her book, *In The SpotLight*. The reader immediately becomes aware that Janet "gets it" on a personal level, having suffered the problem herself at one time. The reader also becomes aware that Janet has the professional expertise to offer a wide array of methods to help the reader tackle the fear of speaking or performing in a most effective way. *In The SpotLight* provides much hope and inspiration for anyone suffering from this limiting fear. The reader is in very good hands as Janet offers hope and help to anyone suffering this fear.

R. Reid Wilson, Ph.D.
Author, *Don't Panic: Taking Control of Anxiety Attacks*

*In The SpotLight* is the book I recommend first to clients with performance anxiety. It offers an array of helpful strategies to deal with public speaking and performance anxiety, presented in a clear, well-organized, easy-to-grasp manner. Written with a compassion based on the author's own experience, this book is destined to become a "classic" self-help reference for performance anxiety.

Edmund Bourne, Ph.D.
Author, *The Anxiety & Phobia Workbook*

*In The SpotLight* is a must read! Janet Esposito has taken a problem shared by many, and experienced by most as shameful, and provided a wonderful set of strategies to overcome it. Janet offers a unique contribution to the field. She integrates the powerful techniques of motivational enhancement and self-development with cognitive behavioral methods to produce perhaps one of the most powerful treatment formulas for social anxiety and speaking phobias. It is a pleasure to read Janet's book and I expect that it will help anyone who reads it and uses it! I believe that if you read *In The SpotLight*, you will need no other book on this topic.

Andrew Magin, Ph.D.
Director, The Connecticut Center for Anxiety Disorders

Self-expression is the most basic of human needs. Some of us, however, become paralyzed by anxiety and fears and are unable to communicate or perform effectively in public settings. Janet Esposito's book can help readers transform their previous negative experiences into golden new opportunities in sharing themselves through self-expression. A must read for anyone who fears public speaking and performing!

Dr. David N. Greenfield
Author, *Virtual Addiction: Help for Netheads, Cyberfreaks, and Those Who Love Them*
CEO, The Center for Internet Studies
Past President, The Connecticut Psychological Association

*In The SpotLight* is a real gift to people experiencing any degree of fear or discomfort in speaking or performing in front of others, either in formal or informal settings. Janet Esposito demonstrates sensitivity, wisdom, and passion in guiding her readers on the path to overcoming their fears and discovering a new-found freedom and power in self-expression. Her enthusiasm for her topic makes for easy and lively reading. You will want to read *In The SpotLight* if you have any anxiousness in speaking or performing in front of others!

Sharon McQuaide, Ph.D.
Assistant Professor, Fordham University Graduate School of Social Service

*In The SpotLight* should become a handbook for people in the performing arts as well as those who are interested in succeeding in other occupations. Its exercises are a guide to developing communication skills that are essential to all relationships, both professional and personal. Janet Esposito has done a tremendous service to those whose potential has been limited by their social anxieties.

Cathy Lipper, M.S.W., D.C.S.W.
Adjunct Professor, Western Connecticut State University

# Overcome Your Fear of
# Public Speaking and Performing

Janet E. Esposito, M.S.W.

*Published by*
*Strong Books – Publishing Directions, LLC*

First Edition
Second Printing 2001

All orders and inquiries for *In The SpotLight* should be
addressed to:
In The SpotLight
PO Box 494
Bridgewater, CT 06752
(860) 210-1499

Copyright ©2000 Janet E. Esposito

All rights reserved. No part of this publication may be repro-
duced in any form, or by any means, without the written
permission of the author. Published and printed in the
United States of America by Strong Books – Publishing
Directions, LLC.

Published by Strong Books – Publishing Directions, LLC
615 Queen Street
Southington, CT 06489

ISBN 1-928782-07-8

Library of Congress Catalog Number: 00-132542

## Dedication

To my wonderful husband Rich, who always believed I would write a book, and to my delightful Golden Retriever Celia, who has always inspired my creativity and joy.

To my Aunt Pat, for her generosity and wisdom, I give my deepest thanks.

_____DISCLAIMER_____

This book is intended for informational and educational pur-
poses only. It is not meant to provide counseling or psy-
chotherapy, nor to provide any medical advice. If you find that
any of the material in this book creates significant distress,
please contact a professional immediately. Also be sure to consult with your physician if you choose to take a medication or
herbal product to help you with your anxiety symptoms
associated with speaking or performing.

## Acknowledgments

I would like to express my gratefulness to the many people who have supported and encouraged me in the process of creating this book. First, I would like to thank the class participants who were willing to share their own experiences in this book to help others. I would also like to thank all of my class participants for their courage in taking the step to help themselves overcome their fear and for their enthusiastic response to my course. I would like to thank Rich and Ceila for giving me all of the uninterrupted time I needed to devote my attention to my writing. I would like to thank David Greenfield, Ph.D. for holding me to my word that I would start a course to help people who have fear of public speaking or performing, which ultimately led to my writing this book. I would also like to thank David for reading and reviewing my book. I would like to express my deep appreciation to Andy Magin, Ph.D. for taking the time to read and review my book and for the incredible acknowledgment and words of encouragement. I would like to thank Cathy Lipper, L.C.S.W. and Sharon McQuaide, Ph.D. for their generosity of time and their feedback in reading an early draft of my manuscript and in reviewing my book at its completion. I would like to thank Roberta Buland, my editor, for her superb editing and her belief in my work. I am also very thankful to Rose Esposito for her helpful comments in reading the final draft. I want to express deep appreciation to Brian Jud, who showed confidence in my book from the start and who walked me through the publishing process with much patience. I would like to acknowledge Pam Redmer for her patience and skill in creating an outstanding logo for my company, which was also used on my book cover. I would also like to thank Tom Tafuri for his generosity of time and talent in creating the design for my book cover. I am grateful to Deb Polydys for her expert guidance in developing all aspects of my company, In The SpotLight, LLC. I want to thank my coaches William and Farah for their unending belief in me and their holding me accountable to the high standards I set for myself. I also want to express my deepest appreciation and gratitude to Tony Robbins for his tremendously inspiring and transformational work, which has allowed me to find the power inside of me. Finally, I want to thank all of the people who expressed interest and enthusiasm about my work and who validated my own excitement about writing this book.

## About The Author

Janet E. Esposito, M.S.W., is a licensed clinical social worker. Janet is the president of In The SpotLight, LLC, a company devoted to helping people overcome stage fright in the areas of public speaking and performing. She created the *No More Stage Fright* workshop in 1998 to give people hands-on experience in learning and applying methods to get beyond the limitations of fear related to speaking and performing in front of others. Her workshop has also been helpful to those who experience any type of social anxiety in relating to others. In addition to leading workshops and refresher classes, Janet offers consultations and coaching by phone, in person, or by email for people wanting individual attention and support in working to overcome their fear of public speaking and performing. Janet is also available to businesses on a consulting basis and for on-site workshops. Janet has also released a CD entitled, *In The SpotLight – Guided Exercises to Create a Calm and Confident State of Mind, Body, & Spirit While Speaking or Performing* as a supplement to her *In The SpotLight* book.

Janet has been a practicing psychotherapist for over seventeen years. She has been in private practice for the last eleven years. Janet's specialties have included helping people overcome stage fright and other anxiety problems, personal performance coaching, stress management, and couples counseling. Janet is a graduate of Smith College School for Social Work.

You can contact Janet by phone at 877-814-7705 (toll free) or email her at *jesposito@performanceanxiety.com.* You can also visit her web site at *www.performanceanxiety.com.*

# Table of Contents

## Chapter One

## *Coming Out Of The Closet*

I never imagined I would be writing a book until a few years ago, when I came out of the closet about my fear of public speaking. Until then I had kept it a secret, sharing my intense fear and dread with only a few trusted family members and friends. I always felt ashamed about having this problem. My biggest fear was that other people would find out how anxious and fearful I was, and they would think there was something really wrong with me. I always wanted to be respected by others, and my deepest fear was that I would lose all credibility and respect if they detected my terror in speaking in front of others. This fear was magnified by what I imagined people would think, knowing I am a psychotherapist. I felt that people would question my soundness as a therapist if I could not even control my own emotional state when it came to speaking in front of a group of people.

I usually felt okay when I was speaking to an individual or only a few people in an informal setting. Sometimes, though, I had a surge of anxiety if I felt intimidated by a particular person or situation, or if I had a moment of self-consciousness about being the center of attention. The real panic, though, came when I had to speak in a more formal setting. This ranged from having to introduce myself in a new situation, such as in a class or seminar, to having to give a formal presentation of any length. My fear escalated even further if I was called upon to speak in front of a larger group of ten or more people, which I had to do from time to time.

Over the years my fear worsened. I was filled with terror and dread whenever I was faced with having to present myself in front of others, even if the spotlight would be on me for only thirty seconds! Along the way, I started to have symptoms of a full-blown panic attack when I knew I had to speak in front of others and there was no way out of it. I felt humiliated by my desperate state and I began to think there was something really wrong with me.

I remember doing all that I could to try to get out of having to speak at meetings or give presentations. While I was able to pull this off many times, there were also times that I could not avoid the inevitable and I had to speak. When I knew I would face a situation where I would have to speak up in a group, or give a formal presentation, I became filled with deep fear and dread for days, weeks, and even months in advance. I would be preoccupied with this dark cloud looming ahead, and it felt as though I were being given a death sentence. Not only was I afraid of speaking in front of others, but I was also terrified of the deep loss of control I felt in my mind and body while I was in this state of intense fear. The fear of my own loss of control and the fear that others would see me so out of control ultimately fueled my fear into panic.

I suffered alone with this fear and experienced a silent terror anytime I faced a situation where I had to speak. I began to organize my professional life around avoiding meetings and other speaking engagements. I was able to do this quite successfully, especially when I went into private practice and was not part of a larger organization. Years went by and I became content in my avoidance. Little did I know I was worsening my problem by the very act of avoidance. All I knew is that it kept me safe and comfortable.

About five years ago I was confronted with having to face my fear again when I joined a partnership in a private practice group. One of the first things my partners proposed was that we make a joint presentation at the local hospital where I used to work. My initial reaction was panic, and I immediately started to think of ways I could get out of it. Fortunately, my next reaction was that I was fed up with my avoidance tactics and finally said to myself "Enough is enough." At that moment I knew that I must try to get over my problem, even though I did not believe I could. I then began to see this presentation as an opportunity to confront my fear once and for all, as I was starting to become tired of the fear standing in my way. In the months prior to the presentation, I undertook a massive effort to learn ways to reduce my panic and anxiety.

When the time came to give my presentation at the Danbury Hospital Grand Rounds, I was delighted to see my success in reducing my symptoms of fear using certain principles and strategies. I felt really encouraged. After that I continued my search for more methods to help myself overcome my fear, and I found myself becoming more and more confident that I could beat this thing. I also began to take more risks to speak up and, while initially very anxious, I was able to tolerate my discomfort and not let it stop me as it had before. I now had certain methods I could use to reduce my fear to more manageable levels. I was no longer feeling so out of control, which allowed me to take more risks. I began to notice a growing trust and confidence in myself and in my ability to speak up, so that my deep fear and dread about speaking began to noticeably lessen. I was both shocked and totally delighted to see this was happening because I had not believed I could really overcome this fear. I had always thought it would be a lifelong affliction that I would have to bear.

As a therapist, I have specialized in helping people who have a wide array of anxiety problems. In recent years I have become most interested in helping people who have phobias related to speaking, as well as performers such as singers, musicians, actors, and actresses who have performance anxiety. In my practice I had helped many people having this type of problem on an individual basis. I began to see results my clients were getting by using the methods that I had used to help myself. I then decided to start a course to teach these methods to groups. In this way, group participants could have a hands-on opportunity to practice the methods while speaking or performing in front of others.

As people took my course and enthusiastically spoke of how helpful the methods were in reducing their fears and inhibitions about speaking or performing in front of others, I decided it was time to share these ideas with others on a larger scale. That is when I decided to write this book, which will be followed by an audiotape series. Helping others like myself who have suffered from this fear has become a driving force in my life. It has become a mission for me to do whatever I can to guide and inspire people to overcome this fear, which has held so many of us back from fully and comfortably expressing ourselves in front of others. This mission has given purpose to my suffering and is an exciting example of turning a problem into an opportunity to help others!

**SUMMARY:**
- Experiencing panic and dread of public speaking or performing often creates feelings of shame and a feeling of being alone in your suffering.
- Continuing to avoid situations of public speaking or performing tends to worsen the fear over time.
- There is a way out of this problem!
- To overcome this problem, you must make a full commitment to do what it takes to learn and apply the principles

and strategies that reduce fear and build confidence in yourself in this area.

- You have the right to fully and comfortably express yourself in front of others and to not be held back by this fear any longer!

**ACTION STEPS:**

- Vow to yourself right now that you will do what it takes to overcome this problem. Decide that you will no longer be held back by this fear and that you have the need and right to fully and comfortably express yourself in front of others!
- Set aside regular weekly time to read this book and do the exercises. Make it a priority to schedule the time for this. Vow to yourself now that you will complete this book and not allow other things to get in the way.

**Chapter Two**

*You Are Not Alone*

The fear of public speaking has been reported to be the number one fear of American adults. You may have heard the joke that most people would rather be in the casket than have to give a eulogy at someone else's funeral!

While the surveys have focused on public speaking, many performers face a parallel fear related to the similar issue of being the focus of others' attention and having their performance evaluated. Given the similarities in the way the fear is experienced, and in the methods used to reduce performance anxiety for both, I will be making reference to both speaking and performing throughout this book. Performers who have attended my *No More Stage Fright* classes have been equally helped by the methods used, which will be outlined in the following chapters.

While most people experience some degree of stage fright, there is a big distinction between those people who have the typical butterflies in their stomachs and report that the antidote to their fear is to be well-prepared and rehearsed, and those of us who experience dread, terror, and panic at just the thought

of speaking or performing in front of others. Being well-prepared and rehearsed does little to reduce the intense fear for
those of us who have a much stronger case of stage fright. For
us, the fear goes much deeper. It is a feeling of being emotionally unsafe when being exposed and vulnerable in front of others. We have come to mistrust ourselves because of the loss of
control we have experienced in our minds and bodies. Our
fear often gets worse, rather than better, as we do more speaking or performing over time. The old advice of "Just be well-
prepared and you will do fine" does not work for us. It makes
us feel even more alone and misunderstood.

You are definitely not alone. Most of us who have this high
level of fear go to great lengths to try to hide it because we feel
so ashamed of it. I was able to hide my fear pretty effectively
and people were shocked to hear I suffered from this problem.
I have always been seen as an outgoing, well-spoken, and confident person. There are many people who appear this way
who are secretly suffering! There are also many people who
tend to be shy and socially uncomfortable who are terrified of
being called upon to speak in front of others.

A study based on 1998 Census data done by the National
Institute of Mental Health (NIMH) on the prevalence of different types of Anxiety Disorders estimated that 5.3 million
American adults between the ages of eighteen and fifty-four
have a Social Phobia. Fear of public speaking and performing
falls within the category of Social Phobia if it meets the criteria
of creating significant distress for the person or interfering sig-
nificantly with his or her occupational, academic, or social
functioning. Most of us drawn to seek out help for this problem suffer deep distress and end up feeling very helpless in the
face of this inner struggle. For most of us, this problem has also
limited us professionally, academically, or socially. It has
stopped many of us from completing higher education, from
going into certain careers, from pursuing opportunities for professional advancement, from expressing ourselves in meetings

and gatherings, or from pursuing other things of importance to us when it might involve being put on the spot to speak or perform in front of others.  Fear of public speaking and performing often takes a big toll on our self-esteem and leads us to feel some degree of inadequacy and inferiority, especially when we compare ourselves to others who seem able to speak or perform with ease and confidence.

My purpose in discussing this problem as a Social Phobia is not to have you label yourself as a "Social Phobic" but, rather, to help you better understand the type of problem you have.  Fear of public speaking and performing does not reflect a character flaw or personal weakness.  It is one type of phobia within a larger category of anxiety problems.  While you may feel this is the worst problem you could possibly have, I assure you it is not.  There are people who are severely impaired by a range of problems with anxiety, depression, and other emotional challenges.  While I do not mean to minimize the problem, as I am well aware of the intense suffering and limitations it can create, it is also important to get some perspective on where the problem lies in the range of emotional challenges that people face in their lives.

One of the essential features of a Social Phobia is a marked and persistent fear of one or more social or performance situations in which embarrassment may occur.  Being exposed to a situation like this creates an immediate anxiety response and often leads to a panic attack.   Most often, the social or performance situation is avoided if at all possible and, if not possible, it is endured with dread.  People with this fear are afraid others will judge them to be anxious, weak, "crazy," or stupid.  Marked anticipatory anxiety generally occurs, often far in advance of the anticipated speaking or performance event.  Other features that someone with a Social Phobia may experience are oversensitivity to criticism, negative evaluation, or rejection; difficulty with being assertive; and low self-esteem or feelings of inferiority.

While some people with a Social Phobia have a general feeling of low self-esteem, feelings of inadequacy, or social unease, there are others who generally feel good about themselves, both professionally and personally, and who are skilled and at ease in many social situations.  For the latter group, having this problem feels like a real contradiction to how they normally see themselves and to what others expect of them, based on their generally high level of functioning.  This was true in my case and led me to feel even more afraid that others might detect my problem, causing me to lose all credibility and respect in their eyes.  Part of my own healing from this problem happened when I came out of the closet about my problem and I did not experience any feeling that others looked down upon me or treated me any differently.  Quite the contrary, people respected my courage for working on this problem and not allowing it to stop me from advancing professionally any longer.

You may be questioning why you have this type of problem, as I often did.  While there are no easy answers to this question, there is almost definitely some combination of nature and nurture at play.  Many of us who have this problem tend toward being more anxious, which likely has some biological underpinnings.  Even more significant for many of us are some life experiences along the way that have created a deep fear of loss of control and a loss of trust in ourselves and often in others as well.  To try to compensate for these feelings, many of us have strived for perfection in order to try to control our world.  Some of us may, instead, have given in to feelings of helplessness and passivity in response to feeling a loss of control.  In either case, there is generally a deep-seated feeling of not being good enough, of being deficient or defective in some way, or of being different from others in a way that will not be accepted by others.  This creates a feeling of shame and a fear of embarrassment and humiliation in exposing your true self in front of others.  There is also a loss of belief and trust in yourself and in others and a feeling of not being emotionally safe to show your true self. These feelings are often not within your conscious awareness. The feelings that you are more aware of are the intense discomfort and self-consciousness at being the focus of attention and the fear that others will be able to see through you and see all of your fears and perceived inadequacies.

You may wonder: So how did I get this way? For some of you, there may have been obvious things that have happened in your life history that created these types of feelings and for others, it may not be so clear. We will explore this further in Chapter Nine to help you become more connected to the source of your fear. It is important to know that there are reasons why you have this fear and that it does not reflect a character flaw or weakness. Understanding its origins and how it may have taken hold in your life is generally helpful in coming to greater self-acceptance about having the problem. While this understanding is helpful, it does not remedy the problem for most people. There are many other methods to use to reduce the hold that this problem has over your life.

**SUMMARY:**
- You are not alone. Fear of public speaking is reported to be the number one fear in surveys of American adults. Many people with this fear try to keep it hidden and suffer in silence.
- There is a parallel fear among many performers who experience a similar fear related to being the center of attention and having their performance evaluated. The methods we will discuss work for anyone with performance anxiety.
- There is a distinction between those with mild to moderate fear and those of us whose fear is far greater and not lessened by preparation and practice alone.
- People suffering from high levels of fear of public speaking or performing generally have a condition called Social

Phobia. People with Social Phobia have a marked and persistent fear and avoidance of social or performance situations in which embarrassment may occur.

- This problem does not reflect a character flaw or weakness. Many capable and accomplished people suffer from this problem. There appears to be a combination of nature and nurture at play, which creates the source of this problem.

## ACTION STEPS:

- If you are like most people who have this problem and have a feeling of shame about it, start right now to shift the meaning you have attached to having this problem. You are probably thinking of this problem as a weakness or failing on your part, and that you should not have this problem and should have been able to beat it by now. Instead, I want you to think of this problem as a form of anxiety that has its roots in both a biological predisposition and your earlier life experience. You have become overly sensitized to being the focus of attention in a situation of performance and evaluation by others. I would like you to have compassion for yourself rather than judge yourself harshly for having this problem. Having this problem is not a statement of your strength of character as a person. It is a function of a negative conditioning process that continues to be reinforced by fearful thinking and avoidance behavior. It is not your fault that you have not been able to overcome this problem on your own. Even the most intelligent and successful people have had difficulty figuring out the solution to this problem on their own.
- Vow that you will stop the cycle of frustration, disappointment, and anger toward yourself for having this problem. Instead, you will work to increase your understanding of the challenges you face and develop compassion toward yourself. Decide that you will never put yourself down again because of having this problem.

## Chapter Three

### *Kindred Souls*

As I have been giving my *No More Stage Fright* classes, I have seen the tremendous healing power that happens when people come together and share their experience with this problem. People start to realize they truly are not alone when they see others who share their fear and all of the feelings associated with it. They start to feel not so different or unusual, and they start on the path toward self-acceptance. In my classes, a deep bond is created as participants quickly recognize that we are all kindred souls sharing a common life struggle in search of a solution.

I would like to introduce you to some of the people who have taken my class. Each had suffered with the fear of public speaking or performing for years. These are their stories before they took the class. These people have come to the class from many different locations throughout the country. The common threads they share are their experience of intense fear and avoidance around public speaking or performing and their equally strong desire to overcome this problem. While I have changed their names for the sake of confidentiality, I have captured their experiences in their own voices.

**Steven C.**

Steven is a 30-year-old single male who has a Bachelor of Science degree in engineering. He is now employed as an environmental engineer.

Steven has quite effectively avoided speaking situations over many years. When he has to speak, he usually suffers extreme anxiety for a day or two ahead of time. The night before, he is hardly able to sleep. When he does manage to doze off, he wakes up in a cold sweat having a nightmare about how badly the speaking event may go. A few hours before the event his heart starts to accelerate and the closer the event gets, the faster his pulse beats. His mouth becomes extremely dry and as the time comes closer he starts to tremble. He fears the trembling might take over his whole body. During the speaking event, his mind races in a negative cycle, seizing any negative thought and blowing it way out of proportion.

Steven's fear began during his freshman year of high school. He was in a college prep class that required him to do a three-to-five minute presentation in front of the class while it was being videotaped. Steven does not remember feeling anxious in anticipation of doing this, but the second he got in front of the video camera and the bright production light came on, he froze. He says he thinks this is when he had his first anxiety attack where his heart started to race at an "incredulous pace." His face flushed and he could feel sweat beading up on his forehead. He states, "I completely lost all sense of being in control and ended up fumbling and stumbling through the presentation. I felt mortified." He felt that his trouble with the presentation made him completely inferior to everyone else. Prior to that he had been outgoing and loved the attention of having leading roles in class plays and reading out loud. After the episode, he completely shied away from any public speaking. While he still fit in socially and was a sports star, student council member, class officer, and top student, he always found ways to avoid speaking in public.

After high school Steven attended a prep school for the Naval Academy. He had hoped the military might help him to combat his fear and build self-confidence. Instead, he wound up dropping out because he had to face situations where he was required to do public speaking. He covered up the real reason for dropping out by coming up with some viable explanation for why he left. "This had to be the low point of my life and I felt like an absolute failure."

After taking some time off, Steven enrolled in a university. While there, he never attended the first classes in which he would have to introduce himself to the class. He never took a class in which he had to give a presentation. He says, thankfully, engineering majors were able to get away with not taking a speech class. If that were not the case, he thinks he might have dropped out. He excelled academically but was somewhat reserved socially, fearful that someone would discover his fear of public speaking.

Steven planned to go on to graduate school and was able to line up a prestigious research fellowship at a leading university. While he was very eager to go, he faced the problem of having to present his research to the faculty, other graduate students, and "reps" from private businesses. Faced with this dilemma, he turned down this outstanding opportunity and did not go to graduate school. He says, "This topped my previous failures as the newest low point in my life."

Steven recognizes that this problem has had a significant impact on his life. He says he developed a well-established pattern of "taking the easy way out" by completely avoiding any and all public speaking situations. He willingly took lower grades in high school in order to avoid giving a presentation. He would take a zero on an oral report rather than give the report to the class. He has passed up two excellent educational opportunities, the Naval Academy and graduate school, because of this fear. Professionally he has "coasted" rather than more aggressively pursuing promotional opportunities. He would never share his fear with anyone and felt like he was "living a lie."

Steven says he has always had a problem with perfectionism. He felt as though he would look completely foolish if he stuttered or lost his thought during a presentation. He thought it was unacceptable not to be "completely cool, calm, and collected." Steven says he had a complete pattern of negative thoughts, "What if this? What if that?"

Both of Steven's parents are alcoholics. Looking back, Steven felt nothing was ever good enough and that he had to do everything perfectly in order to please them. In spite of his accomplishments, Steven continues to find himself battling self-doubt. He thinks he has magnified the problem over the years by not having the courage to actually try to tackle public speaking engagements. After the initial "euphoria of escaping," shame would inevitably set in.

### Julie R.

Julie is a 36-year-old married female with a Bachelor of Fine Arts degree. She works as an advertising art director.

Julie says that when she speaks to a large group she goes into "serious panic" the day before. She becomes dizzy and short of breath. Her heart races and she stops thinking rationally. As the presentation gets closer, the panic comes in "waves." As the waves subside, she becomes rational and strong again - until the next wave. Julie says "timing is everything." If she starts speaking just after a wave, and has a chance to catch her breath, she is capable of giving "a fabulous presentation."

Julie had done advertising presentations for years, as well as teaching college classes, and she had never been nervous. As a child, she had always been in school plays and sung in front of hundreds without a problem. Julie had always loved being on stage. Suddenly, out of the blue, she was speaking in front of a group of students and had her first anxiety attack. Ever since then, Julie has felt panic. Her panic usually happens only in front of large groups of people that she does not know. She has no idea where this fear came from, as performing and presenting in front of others was something she always enjoyed doing.

Julie says her problem has only interfered in her life privately. She states, "I became very afraid of presenting because the panics are true hell." But people do not see her inner panic, and her peers have told her she is an excellent presenter. She says it does interfere with her feelings of self-worth. When she became vice president of her company, she questioned how she could be worthy if she couldn't even get up in front of a group of clients. She felt she did not deserve it.

The only time Julie experienced this problem outside of her work setting was at her wedding. Thirty-five of her closest family members and friends were staying in a bed and breakfast for four days of picnics, sporting events, and big dinners. She says, "These were the people who were closest to me than anyone else in the world." She had friends from as far back as fourth grade for her special day. The day before the ceremony, Julie started having anxiety attacks. She says, "This was not about getting married, as you might think, but about getting up in front of all of these people." She was feeling panicked about being "on stage" and the center of attention. She says, "How weird. Especially since I'd just spent days with these people. These were people I'd known my whole life!" Fortunately for Julie, it ended up being the most wonderful wedding ceremony and she did nothing but smile. She was able to forget there was anyone there but she and her husband and she was able to enjoy the day and have fun.

**Austin P.**

Austin is a 29-year-old, married male who has a Bachelor of Science degree in accounting. He currently works as controller for a medium size retail company.

Austin describes his symptoms as immediate panic upon thinking of any event that would involve him performing in front of a large group. He says he has even had panic attacks watching others perform. These panic symptoms have included a fear of "losing my mind," very cold hands and feet, numbness in his face, pain in his chest and legs, a feeling of confusion and "being disconnected with the world." He says these symptoms have intensified to "incredible levels" up until the actual point of performance. He has experienced a pounding and racing heart, a cold sweat, and intense panic that has made him feel as though he would pass out. His thoughts constantly revolved around failing and the shame associated with not performing up to others' expectations of him. If he was able to get the courage to perform, he generally was able to calm down after the first thirty seconds of a trembling voice and an inner voice telling him he was going to "lose it" in front of everyone. Generally, after these first thirty seconds, these feelings lessened enough to allow him to think clearly and perform.

Austin describes his fear as becoming much worse after he left college and entered the business world. As a child and young adult, he loved performing in front of audiences and was often in the theater, on sports teams, and used to being a leader of groups. However, an intense desire to succeed, a competitive nature, and "an unnatural fear of failure" seemed to show itself as he took on more and more responsibility at work. "One day, out of nowhere, I had a severe panic attack and pretended I needed to leave a meeting due to illness." This had occurred several times since that first episode, and he had become obsessed and consumed with when the next panic attack might strike.

Austin believes his fear has affected all aspects of his life during the last couple of years. At work, he has avoided situations in which he might be asked to present to a large group.

He experiences guilt about this because his job requires these skills. He says, "Pretending to be capable of performing on a moment's notice can be debilitating." His confidence at times is very low, and this has affected his relationship with his family and friends. Although he feels he has done his job well up to this point and has received great reviews and large raises, his fear of public speaking has caused him to be depressed and has "really changed my personality." He says, "The guilt and shame have made me miserable."

Austin says that the source of his fear has come from his strong desire for acceptance and his fear of failure and competitive nature. Much of this, he believes, was instilled at a very young age by his father. He recalls feeling that he needed to be the absolute best at everything in order to gain his father's acceptance. He also believes these personality traits go much deeper than his upbringing and he speaks of being born a very sensitive person. He has always been a person who needed to be liked by everyone and who has measured his successes and failures by what people think of him.

### Isabel M.

Isabel is a 39-year-old single female. She has completed an undergraduate degree and is now the employment manager of a technology company.

Isabel describes the pre-event anticipatory symptoms as "awful," including tremendous anxiety, inability to sleep, extreme visions of the worst possible failure and rejection, and shame and embarrassment at her inability to deal with the situation. At the time of the event, the symptoms become more physical, including "a thundering heart," difficulty breathing, dry mouth, neck and face flushing, and an "out of body" sensation.

Isabel has had this fear as long as she can remember. She has never had "a public speaking disaster," although she has continued to reinforce the fear over the years through "lots of carefully crafted avoidance behaviors. It got to the point that all I had to hear was the word presentation to evoke an anxiety response, even when it wasn't my presentation!" She says the irony is that, in general, she is a pretty good communicator, and the feedback she gets from others on her presentations has always been very positive.

Isabel feels the fear has had a significant impact on her life. She believes it has held her back somewhat at work, but not in any obvious or irreparable way. She has been reasonably successful thus far, though she says, "I will never know how much further along in my career I could be if I did not allow this fear to limit me." She says she is now at a point in her career where she has to "conquer this fear" in order to progress any further.

She feels the biggest impact has been on her self-esteem. She tends to be too self-critical and has allowed this very common fear to fuel tremendous feelings of self-doubt. She has come to view this as her "biggest character flaw." In addition to the fears, she feels as though she has "a secret" to keep, which becomes a burden itself, and that she has failed herself by not addressing this problem earlier in life. The self-criticism around all of this has dominated her self-evaluations and has led to a level of self-doubt that is out of proportion to the problem itself. She states, "Basically, I had lost perspective."

Isabel says that she never had a triggering event that started the cycle of fear. She believes, for her, that it is tied into being a bit of a perfectionist. She has a difficult time accepting anything less than perfection from herself, which she knows is "absurd." She believes that an unwillingness to accept imperfection in herself probably started the fear, and then years of avoidance behaviors have reinforced it.

### Jim B.

Jim is a 51-year-old married male with a Bachelor of Fine Arts degree in graphic design. He currently works as a technical writer.

Jim says that the anticipation of speaking events could bother him up to a week before the actual event. Symptoms immediately before speaking often include a dry mouth and an increased heart beat, as well as a general feeling of panic. While speaking, he often has felt he is on "the edge of losing control." In the worst situations, he says, "My shaky voice would betray me and people would look at me with concern or, worse yet, pity." Sometimes he would do reasonably well despite his anxiety. After these times Jim says he would always feel "a profound sense of relief." Too often, though, he found himself frustrated and depressed afterward.

Jim says he has had this anxiety ever since he started elementary school, but he usually thinks of a bad experience in grade school as the starting point. His fear was greatly increased when his second grade teacher criticized his show-and-tell story in front of the whole class. Jim now says the teacher must have been having a bad day. He doesn't remember her exact words, but the effect was "devastating."

Despite all the anxiety, he has made some progress over the years. For example, as a teenager he remembers having extreme difficulty initiating a phone call, while now it is only a problem occasionally. Over the course of his education and career, he has had a number of successful experiences with meetings and presentations and has felt good about those experiences. On the other hand, he says he has also had "some real disasters, at least in my own mind."

Jim says his career has sometimes been limited by the judgement of others, as well as by his own lack of self-confidence. He believes some people may equate fear of public speaking with general incompetence. As a result, he finds himself not always giving himself credit for the things he has accomplished. He says, "the problem can do major damage to your self-esteem if you let it."

Jim now realizes that his father has also wrestled with this problem throughout his life, although he had never said anything to Jim about it. Jim believes he may have inherited a tendency to feel this degree of anxiety.

Another factor while growing up was the way Jim's older brother treated him. He often criticized what Jim said and seldom gave him credit for having any worthwhile thoughts. This became a way of life in his childhood. It got so bad that as a teenager, he could hardly talk to his brother. When Jim was in his thirties, his brother actually apologized for his behavior, confirming for Jim that he did not imagine these experiences.

### Kathryn M.

Kathryn is a 39-year-old married female currently enrolled in a university pursuing an undergraduate degree in psychology and sociology. Her present occupation is that of a private investor.

Kathryn says she had done almost anything to avoid speaking in public. She says she was fairly successful at avoiding it but that "the cost was an unfulfilling life." When it was necessary for her to speak in public she would feel a sense of dread and "almost panic" for days ahead of time. She would imagine the audience was thinking the worst of her, even long after she had finished speaking. "I would worry that the audience wouldn't like me or what they might say about me. I always felt I couldn't please them." Her physical symptoms included shortness of breath, sweating, shaking, dry mouth, thick tongue, and ultimately, "a loss of reality," of not being aware of her surroundings, or of what she was saying. While speaking she would feel as if all the eyes in the audience were focusing on all of her "self-perceived imperfections and flaws."

Kathryn says she has had this fear for most of her life but that it has become worse with time. As she has grown older, there are things she has wanted to do and the fear has hindered her. It has kept her from advancing in life, professionally, academically, and personally. She quit one job because it meant speaking to large groups of sales representatives. She avoided taking specific college courses where oral reports were required. She has passed up learning and social opportunities which required her to speak to groups of people.

Kathryn says the source of her fear probably comes from her childhood. Her mother always criticized and her father never praised his children. She says what is interesting is that the symptoms she has during speaking correlate with her childhood experiences: the fear that people are focusing on her imperfections, that she won't be able to please others, and the fear that "the physical symptom of dry mouth will literally keep me from speaking my opinions."

## Reggie D.

Reggie is a 30-year-old married male with a Master of Science degree and is now pursuing a Master of Business Administration (MBA). He currently works in a large pharmaceutical company as a clinical scientist.

Reggie says his problem seems to be worst when he knows he is required to speak in front of groups, such as having to introduce himself, or participate in seminars or training groups. He says it really doesn't matter if it is in front of "a group of five or twenty-five people," he still tends to have this anxiety. He says from what he has read, the fear is usually brought on by a fear of failing or being embarrassed in front of a group, but he does not necessarily feel that way prior to speaking. "I just seem to get these panic-like attacks prior to speaking. I almost feel like I need to leave the room." While speaking, his symptoms are usually shortness of breath, voice cracking, sweating, and occasional lightheadedness.

Reggie first noticed this fear when he left college and started working. He was not put in a lot of situations where public speaking was required, but these same symptoms would appear as soon as a situation presented itself. It has been about seven years since the symptoms started. As his career has progressed, so has the need to speak in front of people, and so his feelings of fear have occurred more often.

Reggie says this fear has had an impact on his life. His public speaking anxiety has left him embarrassed a few times. He has chosen certain courses at school because they did not require oral presentations. "I have gotten out of talks which I should have given at work and I have taken less risks at work so I will not be put in situations where I will have to do more presenting." He feels embarrassed. Although most people do not know that he has "this tremendous fear," he knows it. He has a really hard time understanding why this fear occurs. "It makes no sense at all to me that I have a hard time introducing myself to a group of peers and sharing my name and some background information." He says that if it was some detailed or controversial talk, perhaps he could understand the fear better.

Reggie says he is not sure how the fear developed. He believes it started when he first joined his company and felt surrounded by older, brighter, more experienced, and more important people than himself. When he needed to speak in public to these people, he thought they would look at him differently. With each anxious introduction or small speaking event, he came to expect the symptoms and his fear increased.

### Suzanne G.

Suzanne is a 42-year-old married female who has a Ph.D. in psychology. She currently works as a therapist in a mental health department of a hospital.

Suzanne said that her symptoms have included a racing heart, dry mouth, shaky hands, blocked thinking at times, and feelings of being extremely vulnerable and inadequate. "When faced with the task of giving a speech, I am afraid that my unusually high level of anxiety will show through and make people in the audience uncomfortable." Following a speech, her emotions vary. Sometimes she feels proud that she faced her fear and sometimes she is "self-deprecating" because she hasn't done as well as she had wished.

Suzanne has always had some performance anxiety in certain situations, but she doesn't think it was unusually high until the time of high school and college. She believes she "fed the anxiety" by avoiding situations where she would have to face her fears. Each time she avoided a situation, she says, "My fear and lack of self-trust grew." She says that her fear was "compartmentalized," which allowed her to speak in some situations with little to no anxiety. It seemed to be the more formal situations and times where there were large groups that created a high level of anxiety for her.

Suzanne says this fear affected her life in a lot of ways, especially because she was coping with the fear through avoidance rather than "facing it head-on." She said that when she anticipated having to face the fear, she would "curb her responses" by drawing less attention to herself, downplaying her true abilities, and withdrawing from activities that she actually wanted to do but was afraid to do so as not to be called on to speak. She says that personally and professionally she has missed out on opportunities and has let people think she is less capable than she really is in order "to avoid the responsibility of having to speak out loud." She has been asked numerous times to take on leadership roles by people who perceive her to be competent and strong. In response to this, she says, "I have clammed up, squirmed out of the limelight, and let less capable people do the job just to avoid the inevitable request that goes with leadership, which is to express myself in front of a group."

Suzanne says that she thinks her problem probably grew in part out of a natural predisposition toward having a little stage fright. It was greatly compounded, however, by certain childhood experiences, including having a parent who modeled poor emotional control and a family situation that taught her to suppress her thoughts and feelings, and "especially my words." She never learned how to control intense emotion and says, "I simply didn't know there were ways to calm myself down." She also carried "too much emotional responsibility" in listening to problems her mother was experiencing and being told, "Don't tell anyone." This caused her to fear that, "Speaking the truth about certain things would somehow harm people I love." She became very guarded about how much she revealed to others. She says her fear and guardedness made public speaking extremely stressful, because "it was hard to hide myself and my feelings when standing in front of a group."

### Michael D.

Michael is a 35-year-old single man who has an undergraduate degree in finance. He currently works on Wall Street in New York City.

Michael describes his symptoms as a racing heart, shortness of breath, and hyperventilation. He would be "scared to death" and do all he could to avoid speaking situations. He believed that if he were to speak, he would "pass out and embarrass myself terribly." He would have general anxiety months before any speaking engagement, which caused stomach problems, tension, and "grumpiness." When it got close to the actual date he says he couldn't sleep at all. "I felt a feeling of utter hopelessness and frustration."

Michael believed he could speak effectively once he got over the initial surge of fear. He turned to medication to try to control the intense symptoms he experienced. He has used Inderal for the heart-related symptoms and another medication to control the hyperventilation.

Michael says that he recalls having this problem as early as age fourteen and probably much earlier because he was always shy. He says the anxiety got considerably worse starting at about age eighteen when, "I became completely useless in speaking situations." He says this has been a limiting factor professionally, resulting in being less aggressive in taking leadership roles at work and in developing new client relationships. He also feels he has continued to experience a general shyness in other areas of his life.

Michael believes his problem stems from a low self-image, as well as some negative life experiences that have reinforced a set of negative beliefs. He also believes he may have a genetic predisposition to this fear because some of his relatives have similar problems. In his college years he remembers situations where he would be very outspoken in debating issues and people resented him as a result. "This made me hesitant to open my mouth the next time." He also refers to heightened racial tension in the late 80s and early 90s, which had an effect both on himself and his family. He says this made him more introverted and generated feelings of suspicion and vulnerability.

**Diana A.**

Diana is a 46-year-old married woman with an undergraduate degree. She currently works as a homemaker, raising her 9-year-old daughter. She has recently resumed her interest in singing and acting and has been in a number of performances over the past year.

Diana says that her symptoms of performance anxiety have included feelings of helplessness, dread, breathlessness, avoidance of preparing for an audition by not learning the material or, sometimes, over preparing for the audition. She has had feelings of being trapped, thinking to herself, "Why was I stuck with an ability that had to be judged by others? Why did I want to be in a profession where rejection was so much a part of the business?" She says she was stuck in "a continual round of fearfulness before auditions, rejection, and giving up because of how hard it was to make what little progress I made." Her thoughts also included imagining an audition in front of an agent or casting director who would be highly critical, cold, and rejecting. She would then experience feelings of shame, humiliation, and hopelessness.

Diana says that stage fright has caused her "so many starts and stops" and interruptions in her development. She began singing lessons in her mid-teens because she enjoyed being in the high school chorus. She wanted to be a good singer so she could get into the madrigal. Her singing teacher made her perform in recitals and sing in festivals that were to be judged. "That was the beginning of the butterflies, but they were not overwhelming fears." Then she performed in church one spring. On that early Sunday morning she had trouble with allergies and she was "very hoarse" and could not sing well. "When I woke that morning, I felt I was in bad voice, but I was so inexperienced I didn't know what to do about it and I didn't think to tell anyone I wasn't in shape to sing." So when she did perform the song, she remembers being "bad all the way through." She feels her mother was beginning "to live through my musical career" and she feels she really let her mother down on that Sunday morning. "I felt dreadful and humiliated after my performance and was terribly embarrassed by what had happened." Diana wishes she could have gotten some reassurance and encouragement from her mother. Instead, her mother ignored her and didn't say a word. She says, "So covered in her own embarrassment was she, that she forgot to be a mom."

Diana dropped out of college after a year abroad in an acting program so she could attend acting school in New York City. Her stage fright caught up with her, and she ended up dropping out of acting school because of the dread of having to audition for jobs after graduation. "I felt such a foreboding that I was doomed to a life of fear and rejection." She got a job as a clerk in an insurance company and took acting classes at night. "I told myself acting was my hobby." She said that soon she had to confront the inevitability of having to audition and she "ran away again" and decided to go back to college and graduate. While in college she was asked to be in a summer theater production. She did do that and felt "encouraged and inspired." She started taking night classes in the city again and pursued an acting career full-time. Diana says, "This time it stuck from ages twenty-five to thirty-seven." She had overcome a lot of her stage fright "by just the desensitizing force of constantly auditioning and taking classes." When she gave up this time, it was because she was not getting the kind of work she was interested in. She switched professions and became a reporter for a weekly newspaper. She left that job when she "burned out" and decided to become a stay-at-home mom. "After I quit the theater, my stage fright grew back like a weed." Recently, she felt the need for the challenge and excitement that acting classes and performing gave her and, over the past year, has been taking singing lessons and getting back into performing again.

Diana now understands her fear of performing as a fear of abandonment. "Because my mother had inappropriate expectations, both artistically and developmentally, of an inexperienced high school girl, she rejected me when I lost my voice before an audience." Diana says she did feel humiliated when she lost her voice in front of the group but that she "could have survived that had I got warm support from my mother." She says that each time she would sing or audition after that incident, "I would relive that initial devastating rejection by my mother and I would re-experience her abandoning me in a helpless state."

### Tuzines N.

Tuzines is a 17-year-old girl who is a high school senior. Tuzines reports that she developed symptoms of stage fright when she had to play her violin in front of others. She would experience "the shakes" and her knees would feel weak. "I would become worried that everyone would see me shaking." She has had this fear ever since she can remember. However, she has had these feelings only when playing alone or having a solo part, but not when she has played her violin as part of a group.  She becomes frustrated with her problem because "it takes away from my performance and I don't seem to be as good of a player as I am."

Tuzines realized she had this problem because she began to turn down offers to play her music.  She says, "I was afraid I would mess up and make a fool of myself."  She would practice in her room with the door closed and wouldn't even come out to play for her family.

I want to thank these class participants for sharing their experiences to allow others to feel less isolated and alone.  We will visit again with each of them in Chapter Eleven where they share more about how they are using the principles and strategies they have learned from my *No More Stage Fright* class to master their fear and not let it stand in their way any longer.

## SUMMARY:
- There are many people of all ages and from all walks of life who experience the fear of public speaking or performing.
- People who have this fear often feel panic when called upon to speak or perform.  Their anxiety also shows up in physical symptoms that lead them to feel a loss of control.  There is often a fear that their symptoms will betray them and allow others to see how frightened they are.
- Rather than experience tremendous discomfort and risk embarrassment in front of others, many people avoid situations of public speaking or performing as much as possible.  This avoidance serves to further reinforce the fear.

## ACTION STEPS:
- When you are feeling very upset with yourself over having this problem, think about the people who have shared their experiences and remember you are not alone.  Vow to no

longer get angry at yourself for having this problem. Remember that you are taking steps to deal with this fear, and know that there is help and hope for you and others who suffer from this problem!

- Vow to yourself to work toward stopping any avoidance behavior you may be engaging in and, instead, to follow the guidelines in this book to reduce the fear and build more confidence and trust in yourself.

**Chapter Four**

*No Guts, No Glory*

Before going on to describe a range of methods to over-come the fear of public speaking and performing, it is important to get a picture of where you are now, both with your experience of fear and your level of motivation to do whatever it takes to overcome this fear. Many people look for quick fixes that they hope will be comfortable and easy. I can not tell you that this process will be comfortable and easy; in fact, I can tell you there will be moments of discomfort as you take more risks to overcome your problem. Any true success in life requires hard work and dedication, and this is no different. What I can tell you, firsthand, is that the principles, techniques, and methods I will describe to you do work, if you use them with consistency and perseverance. Like many challenges in life, what you get out of it reflects what you put into it. I think of the saying, "No guts, no glory." Overcoming this problem has been my biggest challenge and my biggest victory in life, and I can tell you it was definitely worth the effort and the discomfort I experienced.

As I took more risks, armed with all of the tools I had to

manage my anxiety, I grew more confident. This confidence enabled and empowered me to take more and more risks. I now have done things that would have never been possible when I was busy playing it safe. My most recent victory was speaking in front of over one thousand people at a seminar and feeling ease and enjoyment in the process. It was an incredible experience that I will never forget. I am extremely grateful that I have found a way out of this problem, and I am equally grateful to be able to share what has worked for me and for many others who have used the methods I teach.

### Creating True Success

What is necessary for true success, however, is determination and persistence, both to use the methods consistently and to put yourself in situations where you can increasingly take greater risks to be visible and to speak up or perform in front of others. You do not have to dive in full force, but you do need to commit to making slow and steady improvement. I have included a variety of exercises throughout this book and, to get the maximum benefit, I ask you to do these exercises faithfully. Ideally, do them as you go along in your reading and before you move on to the next section. Or you may decide to read the book once over and return to the exercises. In any event, be sure you do them because by doing them, the real understanding and application in your life takes place. If you only passively read this book and do not do the exercises, you will get less than half the potential benefit that this book offers you. Please do not shortchange yourself on this! If you truly want to overcome this problem, it starts right now with your willingness to do whatever it takes to help yourself.

### Starting A Journal

To help support a high level of motivation throughout this process, I would like you to respond to the following questions. I encourage you to write in a separate journal or note-

book as you go through this book, so that you can easily review
your responses to all of the exercises. I also encourage you to
highlight the text or take notes and review this material before
you make a presentation or give a performance. I also recommend that you keep a running Strategies list on a separate
sheet or note-card of the many different methods I will be
teaching you so that you have easy access to a quick review of
them as needed. I strongly recommend that you review this
material on a regular weekly basis over the next few months
because it is so easy to forget the many different methods that
you can use to help yourself. Also be sure to review the list on
a daily basis for the week or two before a presentation or performance. When you regularly review the material, it helps to
keep these ideas in your conscious mind and more easily
remembered when you most need them. Now, please respond
to the following questions in your journal before you read any
further because the answers will influence the rest of the
process of reading this book!

1.  What specific outcome(s) do you want to achieve as a
    result of reading this book?
2.  What do you stand to gain by choosing to give 100%
    of yourself to this effort and doing all of the exercises and
    the recommended action steps (otherwise referred to as
    *playing full out*)?
3.  What do you stand to lose if you choose to put in a half-
    hearted effort and read all or part of the book and do little
    to none of the exercises and recommended action steps
    (otherwise referred to as *playing it small*)? Please be fully
    honest with yourself. Excuses don't count!

The choice is yours. I am not trying to shame you into
making a wise choice, but I am trying to raise your consciousness so you will think about the consequences of your decision.
Whether you do the exercises or not, I trust you will get a lot of

value out of reading this book. I want to support you in your efforts to get the very best possible outcome from this book so you will truly be on your way to overcoming stage fright. I know from my own experience that dabbling in this effort is not enough. We have to be serious about putting in our very best effort if we expect to achieve the best results. That is how I approached this process, and that is what I want for you, too!

**Self-Assessment Of Your Experience With Speaking Or Performing**

To get started in this process, it is good to get a baseline of where you are presently. Please take a few moments to answer the following questions in your journal. You can refer back to this as you progress, as it will give you a measure of how far you have come. Please be sure to give each response ample time and thought.

1. When did your fear of public speaking or performing start and how has it progressed over time?
2. Describe ways in which you have avoided situations that may require you to speak or perform in front of others.
3. What have been your best experiences in speaking or performing in front of others?
4. What have been your worst experiences in speaking or performing in front of others?
5. What types of thoughts, beliefs, and images do you have related to public speaking or performing that create fear and self-doubt in you?
6. Imagine that you no longer feel this fear and that you now have a new-found feeling of confidence in speaking or performing in public. Describe what this new feeling is like for you.
7. What do you want to be doing differently in your professional or personal life when you no longer suffer from the limitations of this fear?

I strongly urge you to share your responses with at least two people you know and make them aware of your effort to help yourself with this problem. Ask them to be a support system to you as you go through the book and have other things to share with them. In my experience, I have found myself most committed to work hard to overcome this fear when I have shared with others my feelings and my intentions to take action to help myself. By speaking the words to others, I hold myself to a higher standard of following through with my commitments to myself.

**SUMMARY:**
*   Overcoming the fear of public speaking or performing takes persistence and determination. The hardest challenges will also provide opportunities for your greatest victories.
*   It is important to motivate yourself to *play full out* to get the very best results from this effort.
*   To get the most out of this effort, you must hold yourself to a higher standard to make and follow through with your commitments to yourself.

**ACTION STEPS:**
*   Write down your commitment to yourself to do what it takes to overcome this fear and the standards you will hold yourself to in this process.
*   Share this commitment with at least two other people who will also hold you to higher standards around taking action to help yourself. Specifically, ask them to hold you accountable to your commitment.
*   Share your self-assessment profile with these two or more people and request their support in being able to talk to them about what you are learning as you progress with this book.

## Chapter Five

### *Fearing The Fear Itself*

People with intense fear of public speaking or performing have usually had the terrifying experience of a panic attack before or during a speaking or performing event. A panic attack is a period of intense fear or discomfort in which at least four of the following symptoms have developed abruptly and reached a peak within ten minutes. The range of symptoms include.

- Palpitations, pounding heart, accelerated heart rate
- Sensations of shortness of breath or smothering
- Sweating
- Trembling or shaking
- Feeling of choking
- Chest pain or discomfort
- Nausea or abdominal distress
- Feeling dizzy, unsteady, lightheaded, or faint
- Numbness or tingling sensations
- Feelings of unreality and detachment from oneself
- Fear of losing control or going crazy
- Fear of dying
- Hot flushes or chills

While the above are the classic symptoms of a panic attack, you may have also experienced other symptoms of anxiety, such as dry mouth, cold or clammy hands, a feeling of a band around your head, or thought blocking. Consider for a moment what your own symptoms of panic and anxiety have been and whether or not they have met the criteria for a panic attack. For those of us who have experienced a full-blown panic attack, it is quite a terrifying event. It generally leads us to feel an incredible sense of loss of control, which further terrifies us and leads us to fear another episode of this. We come to dread this feeling because of the intense discomfort it produces in us, and we try to do anything possible to avoid feeling this way again.

Earlier on in my career, when I was experiencing panic attacks related to public speaking, I felt desperate and did not know where to turn. I was too ashamed to tell people about it so I suffered in silence. Fortunately, I attended a conference on Anxiety Disorders at that time, and I listened very attentively to the discussion on Social Phobia. The thing that helped me the most at that time was hearing that there is a commonly used medication for people with performance anxiety that helps to block the surge of biochemical reactions that lead to a panic attack. The medication that was referred to is Inderal, a type of beta blocker that is generally used to treat patients with heart problems.

As soon as I arrived home I made an appointment with my physician to discuss my wish to give Inderal a try, and she agreed it could help me. It felt to me like a lifesaver at that time because I was regularly having panic symptoms while presenting at a weekly case conference that I attended. I used the Inderal on an as-needed basis and it helped to reduce the intensity of these symptoms so that I did not feel such an awful loss of control over my physical symptoms. The worst symptoms I was having at the time were heart palpitations, shortness of breath, trembling, and hot flushes. I was especially self-conscious about my blushing because it was such a visible sign of how anxious and embarrassed I was.

While the Inderal helped to keep my physical symptoms more in check, I still found myself very anxious, and I was somewhat disappointed it did not do more to eliminate the fear. I knew I had to do more to deal with this problem, so I started to read about Social Phobia and performance anxiety. The reading helped me to understand more about how the fear spirals into panic and the ways that I could begin to control this process. I was very excited and greatly relieved to learn of some other ways in addition to medication that I could use to help myself control these symptoms.

Before leaving the topic of medication, I want to emphasize that if you choose to consider this as an option, it is essential that you discuss this thoroughly with your physician to see if medication is appropriate for you. If you have high levels of anxiety beyond specific performance situations, you may want to talk with your physician about other medications that may be more appropriate for you. There are also herbal products that have helped some people to reduce their anxiety. Before taking any medication or herbal product, always talk to your physician because it is important not to combine certain medications and herbal products.

**The Spiral Of Fear**

I would now like to share with you an understanding of how the fear spirals into panic and specific things you can do to manage your fear so that you have more control.

For various reasons, we have become very sensitized to our fear of presenting ourselves in front of others. Perhaps we had a bad experience, and the associations in our nervous system to that bad experience have conditioned an intense fear response. Or, perhaps we have other issues that make it very scary for us to feel exposed and vulnerable in front of others, and we feel threatened and fearful whenever we are in a situation that calls for more visibility.

We will leave the exploration of the source of our deep fear to Chapter Nine. For now, it is important to recognize that we have an oversensitivity to fear in this area of our lives. Because of this sensitivity, whenever we have fearful feelings arise in any circumstance related to speaking or performing, we tend to overrespond and experience a deep threat related to this fearful feeling, which in essence creates the vicious cycle of fearing the fear itself. Once this patterned response gets conditioned in our nervous system, our response becomes locked in and automatically repeats itself over and over. This repetitive fear response continues to reinforce itself and generally heightens the feelings of loss of control we experience over time.

As we mentioned earlier, for people with a mild to moderate level of anxiety around speaking and performing, their fear tends to lessen with practice and repetition over time. For those with a phobic level of fear, their fear tends to remain steady or increase over time, and they do not seem to similarly benefit from practice and repetition. This seems related to the traumatic feelings associated with loss of control that the person experiences, which continues to be reinforced each time the person is in a speaking or performing situation. This was certainly true for me when I was working at a local hospital and attending case conferences for years. I was amazed to see how my fear increasingly worsened over many years despite the predictable and repetitive nature of my presentations. My fear and anxiety did not desensitize on its own. It required a more conscious and persistent effort on my part to desensitize my fearful and anxious feelings.

Most of us who have this level of fear have come to hate our fearful feelings and dread experiencing the fear related to speaking or performing. As soon as we hear news of having to speak or perform in front of others, we immediately start to tense and tighten up, bracing ourselves for the onslaught of fear. We look for ways to run from the fear, through attempts to get out of the speaking or performing situation or through attempts to dodge our own fear by trying to push it away. Or, we may instead attempt to fight our fear by trying to resist it or by refusing to give into it. None of these strategies really works as a long-term solution, and our feelings of powerlessness and helplessness over this problem usually win out.

As we experience such helplessness and loss of control over ourselves and our problem, we start to have very frightening thoughts and images about what will likely happen to us when we are in the spotlight for all to see. We see ourselves losing our train of thought and being unable to think on our feet; shaking and trembling; gasping for air; appearing like a total fool; losing all of our credibility, dignity, and respect; having others laugh at us; and ending up a shameful, pitiful mess. Wow! No wonder we are terrified. We create nightmarish predictions in our heads that feel very real at the time and lead us to believe that these will become our fate. While most people with this fear will admit that they do not really believe that things would turn out to be so catastrophic, they tend to emotionally connect to these thoughts and images in a way that feels real. These frightening thoughts, images, and predictions create even further terror as we feel increasingly trapped and helpless in a situation where the stakes are high in terms of losing face in front of others. These terrifying thoughts, images, and predictions, whether fully conscious or more subconscious, are very powerful and can almost instantaneously catapult your fear into full-blown panic.

While we may not be able to gain immediate control over our initial feeling of fear, we can regain feelings of control to a large degree by how we think about and respond to our fearful feelings. In talking to people who have more normal levels of fear around public speaking or performing, it is clear that they do not fear their fear. Instead, they see it as a normal and expected part of speaking or performing so they do not fight it or try to run from it. They accept it and often try to use it to enhance their presentation or performance, channeling it into dynamic energy and enthusiasm. If these people created all of the scary thoughts, images, and predictions that we do, and if they really believed the worst was about to happen, I imagine they, too, would create feelings of panic and start on the same vicious cycle that we have experienced.

## Making Peace With Our Fear

One of the first key strategies we must develop is to change our relationship with our fear. We must stop hating our fear and being terrified of this feeling. We need to start to say different things to ourselves when the fear arises. Instead of saying, "Oh no, here it comes again. I can't stand this feeling. What if I can't pull this one off and people see what a basket case I am?" we need to consciously and deliberately start to create a new response to our fear. We need to say things to ourselves that will create more feelings of safety and acceptance and confirm our ability to tolerate this uncomfortable feeling.

The following are examples of some of the ways we can speak to ourselves to create feelings of increased safety and comfort:

- I know this is an uncomfortable feeling, but it is okay that I have this feeling.
- It is not the best feeling in the world, and it truly is not the worst feeling.
- The more I can accept this feeling when it happens, the more I will learn to manage my fear and do specific things to reduce it.
- I'm going to be okay, no matter what happens.
- The fear won't kill me; it is simply an uncomfortable feeling.
- The feeling will come and go from time to time and I can handle it.

You may want to imagine this as riding out a wave. If you resist the wave and thrash about trying to fight the wave or frantically try to get away from it, you will panic and lose your confidence and energy in the process. Instead, imagine yourself relaxing into the wave rather than resisting it, even welcoming the wave as it comes toward you, and riding it out until the wave dissipates naturally. You may want to imagine yourself floating on your back, loose and relaxed, just above the wave as you ride it out. The more we panic and resist what is happening, either with the wave or with our fear, the more power it will have over us. Our feelings of panic and helplessness in the face of our fear lead us to lose touch with our resourcefulness and our ability to handle the challenges that confront us.

Accepting our fear is no easy task for most people. Our survival instincts guide us to try to fight or flee uncomfortable and painful feelings. We have to resist these tendencies because following these instincts leads us to further interpret the situation as one where our survival is in question. In this case, it is our psychological survival more than our physical survival. Once we create meaning that this is a survival matter, our sense of threat accelerates rapidly and automatically triggers off a survival mechanism within us called the *fight or flight response*, which prepares us to fight or flee danger. We will discuss this response further in Chapter Eight, but for now it is important to know that when this response kicks in, it sets off a series of biochemical reactions which inflame our initial fear response into feelings of panic. If, instead, we desensitize to our initial fear response and we are able to tolerate the discomfort of our fear, our minds perceive that this is not a survival threat to us, and our fight or flight response is not triggered in the same way. This leads to a lessening of our physical reactions to our fear. A positive cycle is then started as we no longer have to contend with a massive physical response to our fear, and we no longer feel such a loss of control over ourselves.

### Creating A Safe Place

As we come to accept our fearful feelings and the discomfort they bring, it is important that we watch our focus of attention as we ride out the wave of fear. Surely, if we focus on nightmarish thoughts and images of ourselves losing control, having others laugh at us, or feeling like the biggest fool there ever was, we are going to feel as though we are riding out a tidal wave and are heading for an undertow. Instead, we must consciously and deliberately shift our focus to reassuring thoughts and images that help us to create a safe place for ourselves. The following are some of the things you can focus on to make yourself feel safer in any given moment:

- Visualize yourself playing with your child or pet.
- See yourself being with your favorite person doing your favorite thing.
- Imagine giving and receiving love with a special person in your life.
- Visualize yourself in a beautiful, serene setting, feeling perfectly calm and at peace, a place where you feel the safest you have ever felt in your life.
- Imagine life beyond the speaking or performance event, later that evening, the next day, the next week, the next month, the next year, even the next ten years. See that you have survived this event, that life goes on as usual, and that with some time the event fades from memory and becomes less and less significant in your life. This helps to regain perspective that you can easily lose when you are fearful.

I would now like you to take a moment to vividly imagine each of these scenarios, one at a time. Close your eyes and use all of your senses to create the experience in your mind as clearly as you can, as though you were right there in the actual situation in that moment. If you are having difficulty with visually imaging any of this, then focus on connecting with the experience using any of your other senses that work better for you.

Now, choose the image that creates the greatest feeling of safety for you. Recreate another vivid image of yourself in this scene and anchor the peaceful, safe feeling by using a subtle gesture that is a gesture you do not normally use, such as firmly touching your thumb and third finger together on both hands. Continue to anchor in the gesture as you vividly imagine your safe place, over and over up to ten times initially. The idea here is that if you continue to reinforce the association of the anchor, such as the hand gesture in this case, and the feeling of calm and safety, then later you will be able to use the anchor alone to create a feeling of calm and safety through association to the original visualization. This does take repetition before it takes hold, so continue to visualize and anchor the feeling until you see that the anchor alone brings forth the peaceful, safe feeling.

The other part of creating comfort and reassurance for yourself is to shift your focus away from the scary thoughts and onto thoughts that can build feelings of trust and safety in yourself and your audience. We are often on automatic pilot, thinking thoughts like, "How am I ever going to get through this? What if they see how nervous I am? They are going to think I'm stupid. What if I can't remember what to say and my mind goes blank? What if I can't pull this off? I am going to lose all respect and credibility. I am going to look like such a fool..."and on and on and on. Wow, we really do a number on ourselves! That's enough to scare even the most confident person. We must stop the mental torture of our terrifying thoughts and images if we are to overcome this fear. We can not expect to mentally and verbally abuse ourselves and build trust and confidence at the same time. Just as we worked to mentally change our images, we must also change what we say to ourselves. So instead of thinking thoughts that terrify us, we must think more reassuring thoughts, such as:

- I have the right to be who I am and express myself in front of others.
- I can be who I am and that is good enough. I do not have to be perfect.
- It is okay that I am anxious. I can still speak or perform, even when I feel anxious.
- It is okay if I make a mistake or forget something. This happens sometimes when people speak or perform, and I will simply do the best I can to recall and move on.
- I can handle this. I have handled many challenges in my life, and I have always somehow managed. I can handle this one, too! I'm going to be okay, no matter what happens.

The quality of our self-talk is an essential ingredient in our ability to overcome our fear. I will talk about this topic again in other sections of the book as it is the core foundation upon which to build greater trust in ourselves and our audience. We must adopt a more supportive, affirming way of thinking and speaking to ourselves. This is an important ingredient in changing our perceptions of ourselves and our audience related to public speaking and performing. You may not find it easy to believe in these positive thoughts and images right away because the fearful thoughts and images have been so deeply reinforced in you over time. Initially, you may have to _act as if_ you believe in the more positive thoughts and images and operate as though you believe they are true. Our transformation often begins with a leap of faith in seeing what is possible and in embracing methods that have been helpful to others, trusting that these same methods can work for us, too.

Before we move on to other techniques, I would like you to

write down in your journal five things you can say to yourself to affirm your ability to handle a speaking or performing situation and to build more trust in yourself. You may want to refer to the examples in this section for some ideas. Be sure to write down statements that create positive meaning for you. Do this on a separate sheet in your journal and add to this list as you go along. Ideally, review it daily so you can start to recondition your way of thinking about yourself in speaking or performing situations. At the very least, be sure you review it multiple times prior to any speaking or performing situation. When you are reviewing this list, it is best to speak the words aloud with positive emotion and energy in your body. Doing so will more quickly reinforce a new association in your mind and condition a new response.

**Grounding Yourself**

Another way of reducing fear is to shift your attention away from the intensity of your inner discomfort and to put the focus instead on the people and things in your immediate environment. Focusing on things outside of yourself helps to ground you in the real world and helps to break the cycle of escalation of scary thoughts and images when they arise. In using this method, you would simply look at different concrete objects in the room and label them in great detail to yourself. For example, you might look around the room at one object at a time and say to yourself, "There is a picture on the wall. It looks like an impressionistic style picture. There are two children playing in the foreground and a background image of a blue body of water and a house in the distance. There is a rug on the floor. It is an area rug with an interesting pattern of diamonds and squares. It has four different colors, with the primary color being emerald green. There is Karen. She is wearing a really nice dress. It has five buttons in the front and is a beautiful royal blue color." You get the idea. Continue to look around the room and label details of concrete things only. Do not start to think about what Karen will think of you if she sees how nervous you are!  Stay only with what is neutral and observable.  You will begin to notice a drop in your level of fear when you deliberately shift focus away from a preoccupation with your imaginary fears and your inner distress, and instead pay attention to things that are concrete and emotionally neutral.

This not only grounds you in the real world, but it also occupies your mind so that it makes it harder for the scary thoughts and images to intrude.  I found this technique especially helpful when my level of fear was very high, for example an eight or more on a rating scale of zero to ten, with ten being a full-blown panic level.  It is hard to create reassuring, confidence-building thoughts and images when your fear is flying high and heading off the scale!  This technique helps to bring the fear down to a more manageable level so that you can then begin to use more effectively the method of creating positive and affirming thoughts and images in your mind.

**The Benefits of Deep Breathing**

Another method to start using at the outset is that of deep breathing.  We will review other relaxation methods later, but this is a very basic method to start with and works effectively for most people.  When we are in a state of fear and distress, our breathing automatically becomes more shallow and rapid as part of the fight or flight response because our minds are perceiving we are in danger and need to prepare to protect ourselves.  Breathing in this way then starts a chain reaction of physical responses as our body prepares for danger, which sets the stage for a panic attack resulting from feeling the loss of control in our body.  What we can do for ourselves, instead, is to consciously and deliberately do a deep breathing exercise to override our automatic physical response.

Deep breathing has multiple benefits because it starts a positive feedback loop in the body, giving off the message to the body that we are not in danger and there is no need for an alarm reaction. It also gives us a positive focus of attention, and it leads us to focus on something we can control, thereby stopping the cycle of escalation of fear.

I will describe two methods of deep breathing, and I would like you to take the time now to try both methods and see which one works best for you. Then I suggest you practice this method from one to three times daily so you become familiar with it and are able to use it more readily when you really need it. I practice deep breathing daily, both for the relaxation and the health benefits. Not only does deep breathing relax the body, but it also oxygenates the cells of the body. Because I have practiced it so often, it is now second nature to me and is much easier to use when I am approaching a speaking event. I especially find it helpful when I am driving over to a speaking event or waiting to go onstage.

### Deep Breathing: Method One

Lie down in a quiet, comfortable spot or sit comfortably in a chair. Be sure your clothing is loose and comfortable. Start by closing your eyes and shifting your focus within. Now gently and gradually deepen your breath, breathing in through your nostrils and allowing the breath to gently expand your diaphragm and lungs. As you do this, your belly will naturally expand. Put your hands on your belly to feel this expansion, followed by contraction when you slowly and gently release the breath through your pursed lips or through your nostrils, whichever works best for you. Repeat this from five to ten times, starting to count as you breathe in and out. You may want to start with the count of four on the in-breath, two for the holding breath, and eight on the out-breath. It is generally recommended to breathe out about twice as long as you breathe in. You can change the count to whatever works best for you as there are no magic numbers to use. Also practice deep breathing several times with your eyes open, focusing your attention on some object in the room as your breathe. Most people become immediately relaxed when they do deep breathing. If you become dizzy or lightheaded, stop the exercise until this feeling stops, and resume it again at a slower pace and do not breathe as deeply. Be sure to give yourself a few minutes of breathing normally before you stand up, otherwise you may feel lightheaded or dizzy.

While most people have no problem with this exercise, consult your doctor if you continue to have symptoms of dizziness or lightheadedness. Some people have difficulty deepening their breath because they are used to breathing in a constricted, shallow way. With practice, you should see yourself making progress in breathing more deeply without much effort.

### Deep Breathing: Method Two

Create the same relaxing conditions for this exercise. Lie down or sit in a comfortable, quiet spot. Be sure your clothing is loose and comfortable to allow for your expanding breath. Close your eyes and again put your hands on your belly. This time, start by focusing on expanding your belly as fully as possible without straining. As you do this, you will notice you automatically take in a deep breath. Hold the breath for a few seconds, then contract your belly inward and notice this automatically leads you to release your breath. Breathe out either through pursed lips or through your nostrils, whatever works best for you. Now practice this technique five to ten times, using the count that works best for you. Practice with eyes closed first, and then continue with eyes open, so you become familiar with deep breathing both ways.

Which method works best for you? You may have a clear preference, want to try them both out some more, or alternate between the two. Whatever you choose is fine, just be sure to practice, practice, practice! I can't tell you how many people have told me that the practice of deep breathing has really helped them to reduce their anxiety and to create a feeling of being more grounded. You may also want to practice deep breathing with some slow, relaxing music to pace yourself. You can use this technique in all situations when you are feeling anxious. When you are by yourself, you may want to do it in such a way that you hear yourself breathe in and breathe out. When you are with others, you can do this silently and no one will ever know!

**SUMMARY:**
- Most people who have an intense fear of public speaking or performing have experienced the terrifying feeling of a panic attack. This leads to a deep feeling of loss of control and a dreaded fear of another episode of panic. The fear of another panic episode then leads to a cycle of avoidance behavior, in the hope that panic can be escaped.
- Inderal, a type of beta blocker generally used for heart patients, is a commonly used medication for people with panic symptoms associated with stage fright. The medication blocks the surge of biochemical reactions associated with the *fight or flight response*. The medication does not eliminate all symptoms of fear and, if used, should always accompany other methods to reduce and overcome the fear. There are also herbal products that can help reduce symptoms of anxiety. Consult with your physician if you want to consider the use of medication or an herbal product in helping you reduce the intensity of your physical symptoms.
- People with a phobic level of fear of public speaking or performing become overly sensitized to their own fear response, and they become caught in a vicious cycle of fearing the fear itself. The fear tends to remain steady or increase over time and does not generally benefit from practice and repetition, as it does for others with a milder case of stage fright.

- People with a phobic level of fear generally come to hate their fear and try to resist and avoid it at all costs. This process creates deeper feelings of helplessness when the fear arises, and it gives the fear even more power. People with this fear also tend to create very frightening thoughts, images, and predictions about what will happen to them when they are in the spotlight. This further fuels the fear into panic.

- We need to change our relationship with our fear and give it new meaning. Instead of saying things to ourselves that create feelings of terror and helplessness, we need to start saying things to ourselves that create thoughts and images of safety and acceptance of our fearful feelings. We need to ride out the wave of fear rather than fight it or run from it.

- When we are deeply threatened by our fear, the fight or flight response automatically kicks in as we perceive this to be a matter of survival. When we come to accept our fear and do not resist it or try to run from it, our minds perceive that this is not a survival threat to us and the fight or flight response is not triggered. Our physical reactions to our fear lessen and this starts a positive cycle of regaining control.

- We must consciously and deliberately refocus our attention away from frightening thoughts and images and onto reassuring ones that create feelings of comfort and safety.

- The quality of our self-talk is an essential ingredient in our ability to overcome our fear. We must adopt a more positive and supportive way of thinking and speaking to ourselves to build trust in ourselves. Initially, we may have to *act as if* we believe in ourselves and take a leap of faith in seeing what is possible.

- When we have very high levels of fear, we can use a grounding exercise of focusing on real objects in the room, rather than on our imaginary fears. This focus competes with creating terrifying images and thoughts in our heads so we do not add more fuel to our fear.

- Deep breathing is a very important technique to use to calm your nervous system. It gives your body the message that you are not in danger and it does not need to engage the fight or flight response to protect you from harm. This can start a positive cycle of calming the mind and body.

**ACTION STEPS:**

- Be sure to start your Strategies list and add the different strategies that you learn after reading each chapter. Review these strategies weekly until they become very familiar, and then review them periodically after that to refresh your memory. Be sure to review the list daily for one to two weeks prior to a speaking or performing event.

- Work on developing an attitude of acceptance of your fearful feelings. Consider what you now say to yourself and what you imagine in your mind that fuels your fear. Begin to consider what other thoughts and images you can focus on that will create feelings of safety, comfort, and acceptance of your feelings. Close your eyes and imagine yourself floating above your fearful feelings and riding them out like a wave, without fear or struggle.

- Practice visualizing an image of your safe place and use your anchoring gesture to reinforce the association. Do this daily for ten days. Try bringing back that calm and safe feeling by using your anchor alone. Keep reinforcing the connection between feelings of safety and your anchor.

- Practice the deep breathing exercise two to three times a day, for a cycle of five to ten breaths, for at least the next ten days. After that, continue to practice the breathing at least one time a day so that it becomes second nature to you.

- I highly recommend that you put these strategies into practice within one to two weeks by arranging to speak in front of others, focusing on the methods you have just learned. You may have a situation at work or elsewhere where you can immediately apply what you have learned. Even if you have a ready-made situation in which to practice these strategies, I encourage you to create one with others you trust for extra practice and support. For example, you may want to ask some family members or friends to come together, letting them know you need a forum in which to practice your new skills. Have at least two people present, giving a brief, five-minute talk or performance in front of them. Your focus is on practicing the strategies you have just learned, rather than on giving a stellar talk or performance.

Notice your level of fear and anxiety before and during your talk or performance and how using the strategies reduces your level of fear. If you are speaking or performing in front of friends or family, let them know your purpose and request that they do not give you any critical feedback that would help you improve your talk or performance. Ask them to give you only positive feedback for now. Tell them it must be genuine and not meant simply to boost your confidence. Let them know it is most important to be supportive and to allow you time to master these strategies. It is also a good idea to have yourself video-taped each time you do an exercise of speaking or performing and to review it with a supportive, noncritical attitude. Most people find it reassuring to see that they almost never appear as nervous as they feel inside. If you do not have access to a video camera, you may want to audiotape yourself to hear how you sound, realizing you are still able to speak or perform despite your fear. Remember, you must always be supportive and noncritical when you review yourself on tape, focusing only on what is reassuring and confidence-building.

## Chapter Six

### *It's Not About Me*

The fear of public speaking and performing is created by a lot of self-focusing and internal preoccupation. We are consumed by feelings of fear and self-consciousness, and we worry about what others will think of us. We are especially concerned about what others will think if they see how anxious and afraid we are. We fear that others will think less of us, that they will lose respect for us, and that they will think there is something wrong with us.

The more consumed we become with ourselves, the more psychological distance we create between ourselves and our audience. We lose the feeling of connection with others as we withdraw into ourselves and become preoccupied with our inner state of mind and body. The more we experience a feeling of separation rather than connection with others, the more we experience feelings of aloneness, alienation, and not belonging. We end up with a feeling of being out on a limb all by ourselves without any support from others, which further reinforces our fear.

We make ourselves far too significant with all of this intense self-focusing and concern, which leads to a real distortion in our perception of ourselves and the situation we are facing. We make ourselves far too important and then feel terrified by how important we have made ourselves! We also create a distortion in how we see ourselves when we become overly focused on our feelings of self-doubt, fear, and vulnerability. This focus leads us to pay close attention to all of our perceived inadequacies and deficiencies. In this process, we discount our real strengths and capacities to cope with life's challenges. We wind up feeling a childlike quality of helplessness and powerlessness, and we lose our connection with our more usual adult functioning. I remember many times feeling like a child inside, so terrified and alone, and yet having to think and act like a grownup while others observed me in my role as a speaker. This was a very scary prospect indeed! We will discuss ways to connect more with your adult functioning in the next chapter as this is crucial to feeling self-trust and confidence in your role as a speaker or performer.

The solution to breaking this cycle of negative self-focusing is to take the focus off ourselves and to put our focus on our audience. Our attention needs to be directed toward what we can do for our audience, not on how the audience views us. As a speaker or performer, it is helpful to put our energy into making the audience feel welcome and at ease, as though we are a gracious host or hostess and we are welcoming them into our home. We can do this by building connections with people in our audience, ideally before, during, and after our talk or performance. These connections are built through the warmth and openness in our eye contact, our body language, and our words. These connections are also built when we relate to our audience as distinct individuals, rather than as one large mass of people. When we perceive the audience as a mass (or a mob!), we tend to also perceive that it is a situation of them against me and that they are out to get me. We need to humanize the experience by being more of a real person and allowing the audience to see our vulnerability as a human being, rather than trying to appear as though we are perfect. Ironically, the more you strive for perfection, the more you distance others; the more you allow others to see your realness and your vulnerability, the more you create closeness and connection with your audience.

The other primary focus needs to be on how we can contribute to our audience and make a difference by communicating or performing in a way that brings value to the lives of others. It is important not to fuel self-doubt by thinking you may not have enough to contribute. We all have something of value to give to enhance the lives of others. Your contribution does not have to be monumental! You may have heard the saying, "Love conquers all fear." We need to create a genuine caring for our audience so that we truly want to give of ourselves to better the lives of others. It is in our deep concern and caring for others that we lose our fear as we put the interests of others above our own self-interest.

Rather than being preoccupied with thoughts and images about our fear and our doom and gloom predictions about what is going to happen to us, we need to conserve that precious energy and focus instead on how we can best serve the needs and interests of our audience. Instead of asking ourselves the questions, "How am I ever going to get through this? What are they going to think of me when they see how nervous I am?", it is important to ask ourselves more resourceful questions such as, "How can I best serve the needs of my audience? What can I do that might add the most value to the experience of those in my audience and might make a difference in their lives?"

It is essential that we connect more strongly with our adult selves and our adult capacity to think, function, and cope with responsibilities and demands made upon us. We must step out of a self-centered mindset, which is characteristic of a child's egocentric thinking, where the child thinks he or she is the center of the universe. Instead, we need to re-enter our adult mind-set and be concerned about the needs of others. This happens when we focus on the real purpose of our being at a speaking or performing event, which is to be of service to others to the best of our ability. Our purpose is not to impress people and to show them how good we are. People could really care less about that. They are concerned with their own needs and interests and with getting something of value to take home with them. We are not so important that people will think about us and talk about us endlessly, whether we do a good job or not! We are only important to others in our audience relative to how we meet their needs. Remember, it is not about you! It is about what you can do for others.

The principles I have described for you have made an enormous difference in my life. I have come to understand and integrate these principles into my thinking over the past few years. As a result, I have experienced a dramatic decrease in my level of fear. Using these principles has grounded me more in my adult self and has led me to rise above my self-consciousness and preoccupation about my own performance. I have been able to rise above my concerns about self and to focus more on my purpose and mission as a speaker, which is to contribute to the lives of others. I have found myself much less self-interested and much more loving and caring about others in the process. I now experience an eagerness to connect with my audience, which results in my not fearing my audience. I urge you to embrace these principles and continue to integrate them into your way of thinking about yourself as a speaker or performer. I am confident that this shift in perception of yourself and others will make an incredible difference in your experience with public speaking or performing.

**SUMMARY:**

- Self-focusing and preoccupation with our inner distress increase our fear by creating psychological distance from others, leading us to feel alone and without connection or support.

- We need to shift to being "other focused" and to create a connection with our audience, caring more about our audience than our own self-interest.

- We need to shift our focus away from the concern about how we will be perceived by our audience and onto how we can best serve the needs and interests of our audience.

- We need to ground ourselves in our adult way of thinking and functioning and to connect with our strengths and capabilities, rather than experience ourselves in a helpless, childlike state.

- Our primary focus needs to be on how we can contribute to and make a difference in the lives of others.

**ACTION STEPS:**

- Close your eyes and imagine yourself fully embracing these principles as you anticipate your next speaking or performing situation, whether it be a formal presentation or performance or an informal meeting or rehearsal.

- Further imagine yourself in the speaking or performing situation fully engaged in your purpose of creating value and making a contribution to the lives of others. How you look to others is now insignificant. In essence, you lose yourself as you focus on your higher purpose and mission that come out of your love and caring for your audience. Your sole focus is on how you can best serve your audience and make a difference in their lives.

- Apply these principles in a real speaking or performing situation. Even if you have a speaking or performing situation coming up, first create one with friends and family for extra practice and support. Focus on offering them some information or entertainment that they will find interesting and enjoyable. Choose something that you want to share with them that will have meaning for you and for them. You can make this a brief exercise of about five minutes of speaking or performing. Notice any differences you feel in your level of fear and anxiety before and during your talk or performance, and how it feels afterward. Notice how well you were able to keep your focus on creating value for others, not on how you looked. Continue to practice these principles in other speaking or performing situations and observe how your fear and self-consciousness lessen over time.

**Chapter Seven**

*Creating Beliefs and Self-Talk That Support Us*

People who suffer from an intense fear of public speaking or performing hold negative beliefs about themselves and the audience that are almost never grounded in objective reality. These beliefs create a series of negative predictions of how badly we think things are going to go when we are speaking or performing, which are also not grounded in objective reality. These negative beliefs and predictions arise from our fear; and, because they have such a strong emotional charge, we tend to believe in them. However, if we examine our beliefs and predictions from a rational and logical state of mind, we are most often able to say that we don't really believe all of these awful things are going to happen to us. While we may be able to say this rationally, we still come back to believing in our doom and gloom predictions as though they were true.

Our beliefs and predictions tend to follow our emotions rather than being based in a more rational and reality-oriented view of ourselves and the speaking or performing situation. Once again, this kind of thought process is more characteristic of a childlike way of thinking. Children may create scary ideas in their imagination and believe in these ideas because they feel so scared. This can be seen in the classic *monsters in the closet* and *bogeymen under the bed* images. We create these same monsters and bogeymen in our own heads; and, because we feel so scared, we conclude that our terrifying beliefs and predictions are really true.

We must start to become aware of how our fear grossly distorts our perceptions of reality in public speaking or performing situations. We need to start to identify, and to challenge, our negative beliefs and negative predictions. This process helps to ground us in our adult selves, where we are more connected to objective facts than to childlike imagination. When we are connecting to our adult way of thinking, the picture is not so scary. We realize there are no monsters or bogeymen in our audience, or even piranhas ready to swallow us alive! We are then able to create a more rational and realistic assessment of ourselves, our audience, and our purpose in speaking or performing.

Some people have expressed that they are afraid to let go of their catastrophic way of thinking because their guard will be down if the worst case scenario does occur, and then they will not be ready for it. They feel safer by always bracing themselves for the worst that could happen. We all know this feeling. We are so afraid to be caught off guard and to feel a loss of control. The problem with this way of thinking is that by focusing on our worst case scenario, we greatly distort the probability of it happening and the consequences that would follow should it ever happen. If we so strongly believe the worst will happen, we can also generate so much fear about it that the chances of it happening may actually increase. This is referred to as the *self-fulfilling prophesy*, the idea that what we strongly believe in is more likely to come true. For example, if we are so afraid that we will lose our train of thought when we are presenting or performing, we can become so anxious about this that it may set the stage for us to lose our train of thought.

We must be willing to face our worst case scenario in a more adult fashion. We need to assess the realistic probability of it occurring and the realistic consequences that would likely take place. Then we can create a plan of action to prevent it or to handle it, should it actually occur. For example, we may be terribly afraid that we will completely forget everything in our presentation or performance, that we will look like an idiot, and that everybody will lose respect for us and think we are stupid. First, instead of fighting it, we have to resolve to accept that this could happen. While this would certainly be very uncomfortable, believe it or not our life would not be over and we would not be cast off to a deserted island to wither and die! Even if we were to lose our job because of this, which is highly unlikely, we would find another job and would not end up homeless and on the street!

In this example, if we were truly thinking from an adult perspective, we would assess that the probability of forgetting everything in our presentation or performance is very low, that the probability of looking like an idiot is also very low, and that the probability of everyone losing respect for us and thinking we are stupid are similarly very low. We would further assess that the realistic consequences of forgetting all of our material in a presentation or performance is that we would have to apologize to the audience and graciously excuse ourselves. We would probably want to follow this up afterward with an explanation to our boss or whoever hired us to do the talk or performance. We would try to learn from the experience and problem solve regarding what we could do differently to reduce the chances of this happening again. If we had created a plan of action at the outset to deal with the worst case scenario, we could have stopped it from happening. For instance, if we had prepared and rehearsed very thoroughly beforehand, and then had our notes with us (even written out word for word to guide us, if needed), we would have had a backup in the event we forgot what we planned to say or do.

I know someone, named Victor, who had his worst case scenario happen to him when he fainted while preparing to speak in front of a board meeting. While this can be a terrifying thought, what is delightful about this story is that after this experience Victor got back on his horse and continued to speak in front of groups. While he felt embarrassed about what happened, he was not stopped by it. Victor continues to be a successful businessman and is now able to laugh about what happened. He saw that his worst fear happened and he came out of it okay. Now he is even less afraid because he faced his demons and saw that everything worked out in the end. I am very grateful that Victor did not give up in despair. He is a very talented speaker and a solid leader who has much to offer others. He did not use this event to convince himself that he was a total failure and that this would likely happen again if he got up to speak. Instead, he was able to put the event in its proper perspective and to learn from it. He left it behind and moved on.

I am sharing the story of Victor not to scare you, but to reassure you that you will survive and be okay even if the worst happens, which it *very rarely* does! We typically say to ourselves, "What if this happens? What if that happens?" We leave these questions dangling and unanswered. We need to realistically assess the probability of these things actually happening, and to answer the *"What if"* questions with a response based in reality, not based in fear. We can ask ourselves a more resourceful question, such as "What can I do to reduce the possibility of that outcome occurring?" This line of questioning shifts you out of being in a fearful, helpless, childlike state and puts you into the mind-set of a problem-solving, capable adult. As you shift your line of thinking to be more adult-like, you build confidence and trust in your ability to handle the situation capably. This further reinforces more positive beliefs and predictions about yourself that are grounded in objective reality.

**Challenging Imaginary Fears**

To better understand the ways we negatively distort reality, it is helpful to consider the following list of *cognitive distortions:*

- *All or nothing thinking:* You see things in black and white terms. Because you strive for perfection, you see yourself as a failure if your performance is less than perfect.
- *Overgeneralization:* You see a single negative event as a never-ending pattern of defeat.
- *Mental filter:* You pick out a single negative detail and dwell on it exclusively, ignoring contrary ideas or evidence.
- *Disqualifying the positives:* You reject the positive accomplishments or qualities you have to offer.
- *Jumping to conclusions:* You make a negative interpretation, even though there are no definite facts that convincingly support your conclusions. Examples of this are:
- *Mind Reading* - Making assumptions about what other people think about you when there is no definite evidence for this
- *Fortune Telling* - Anticipating things will turn out badly and feeling convinced your prediction is an already established fact
- *Magnification* (catastrophizing): You exaggerate the importance of things and blow them out of proportion.
- *Emotional reasoning:* You assume that your negative feelings reflect the way things really are, leading you to believe "because I feel it, it must be true."
- *Absolute thinking* (shoulds): You have rigid rules and expectations for how you and others should be.
- *Labeling:* You criticize yourself or others by using negative labels such as fool, idiot, loser, and weak if you or others are not measuring up to your expectations.
- *Personalization:* You take other peoples' negative reactions and behaviors personally, assuming they are about you.

The concept of cognitive distortions was written about extensively by Aaron Beck, a pioneer in the field of *cognitive therapy*. This type of approach helps people to identify and examine their beliefs and thought processes and to recognize the ways they may be distorting a more objective assessment of reality. We are all subject to distorting reality, based on our past experiences and the meanings we have created to interpret those experiences. The more emotionally charged something is for us, the more likely we are to distort the objective reality. This is very true for us when it comes to public speaking or performing. Our intense fear leads us to believe and predict things that are not real or likely to happen. For example, common negative beliefs and predictions include:

- I can't do this. This is going to be awful.
- I will look like a fool up there.
- Everyone is going to laugh at me or feel sorry for me.
- I will lose all credibility and respect.
- I should be able to handle this-what's wrong with me?

After becoming aware of our negative beliefs and predictions, the next step is to identify the cognitive distortions in our thinking by referring to the list. Please note that some of these categories overlap. Do not worry about getting the categories just right. The more important point is to start to recognize the ways we are distorting reality and to create alternative ways of thinking that are a more accurate portrayal of objective reality. In this example, we are distorting reality in the following ways:
- I can't do this. This is going to be awful.
  Emotional Reasoning, Jumping to Conclusions - Fortune Telling
- I will look like a fool up there.
  Negative Labeling, Jumping to Conclusions - Fortune Telling
- Everyone is going to laugh at me or feel sorry for me.

Jumping to Conclusions - Fortune Telling, Mind Reading
- I will lose all credibility and respect.
  All or Nothing Thinking, Jumping to Conclusions - Mind Reading
- I should be able to handle this-what's wrong with me?
  Absolute Thinking (shoulds), Negative Labeling

Once we are able to see our own pattern of distortion, the next step is to create a new set of beliefs and predictions based on rational thinking and on a more accurate assessment of objective reality. Using our example, a more rational way of thinking would go as follows:

- I know I can do this even though I feel anxious and uncomfortable.
- Many speakers or performers are anxious and uncomfortable, but they do not look like fools. Even if I feel foolish, that does not mean I look like a fool.
- If people see that I am anxious, they may feel some compassion or concern for me. I can't control what people are thinking, so I need to focus on my purpose and not wonder what they are thinking.
- People tend to be more accepting of me than I am of myself. If someone else makes a mistake or forgets something, I do not automatically lose respect for him or her or think that nothing he or she says is credible, so why should I think others will do that to me?
- It is okay for me to feel anxious. I can still speak or perform and do okay even when I am anxious. I know I will feel less fearful if I stay focused on more positive and reassuring thoughts and images, and on my purpose to contribute to others.

Our perceptions of how we appear to others when we are anxious and fearful tend to be grossly distorted. Time after time in my classes people say they feel so anxious and fearful inside of themselves, yet the group detects little to no anxiety in the way they present themselves. When the class participants are able to see themselves on videotape after the class, they are often amazed to see that they came across far better than they had perceived. This distortion falls into the category of Emotional Reasoning (refer to list), where we think that because we feel strong emotions, we display to others what we feel inside. This just isn't so. Sure, sometimes people do appear very nervous as speakers or performers, but most of us do not portray the intensity of the feelings that are going on inside of us. In fact, we appear calmer than we could ever imagine!

### Creating A New Set Of Beliefs And Predictions

Once we become aware of how we distort reality and, as a result, create incredible self-doubt and mistrust of ourselves and others, it is essential that we create new patterns of thoughts and beliefs that are based in reality. If fact, one of the benefits of being in our adult mind-set is that we can examine our belief system and thought process. We can then make conscious decisions to work toward eliminating negative beliefs and thought patterns that do not serve us. This frees us to adopt a new set of beliefs and thought patterns that works for us and allows us to be at our best. It takes time to let go of our old, familiar way of thinking because it has been reinforced so strongly, often over many years. It also takes time to recondition new, alternative beliefs and patterns of thought because we tend to gravitate toward what we are used to and it often feels risky and awkward to change our ways.

To create change in your belief system, you will need to be patient and persistent in reviewing the new beliefs and thought patterns that you want to adopt. Focus on them over and over to give them reinforcement and strength. You may not believe in these new empowering beliefs and predictions right away, especially if you have not yet built up positive experience to back up your new ways of thinking. If this is the case, you must take a leap of faith and act as if these beliefs and predictions are true. Doing this will allow you to start releasing the power of the negative beliefs and predictions. You will begin to create a new possibility for a more resourceful and realistic way of viewing yourself and others in public speaking or performing situations.

It is worth noting that people who feel confident and at ease with public speaking or performing operate from a very different set of beliefs and predictions about how they will do than those of us who suffer from intense fear. The very beliefs and predictions we have set the stage  for determining how we will behave. If someone believes that he or she is capable and predicts being able to do a good job with a presentation or performance, usually the power of this belief and prediction will lead the way toward the expected outcome. On the other hand, if we believe we can not handle it and predict we will mess up and not be able to pull it off, chances are pretty good that our presentation or performance will suffer from the influence of our negative beliefs and predictions.

It is helpful to talk to people and read stories about people who are successful in public speaking, performing, and other challenging areas of life. Very often you will find that these people prime their minds for success by thinking about and focusing on empowering thoughts and beliefs. To stay in a resourceful state, they refrain from thinking in ways that undermine their self-confidence and self-esteem. We need to use these people as role models and practice the principles that make them successful. That is one strategy I have used a great deal, and it has been immensely effective for me. I have observed, read about, and talked to people who display a lot of confidence and power in their speaking and performing abilities. I learn what they do to create this resourceful, empowered state of mind, and I adopt similar attitudes and behaviors. Sometimes I think about a particular person and imagine being that person and facing a public speaking or performance challenge. What would I be thinking about and doing to prepare myself to be at my best? I step into the shoes of that person and act as if I were him or her in the moment, connecting with feelings of strength and power through identification with the principles that person lives by. I find this strategy always helps me to connect with a deeper source of power within myself and allows me to experience a renewed feeling of confidence and strength.

**Banishing The Critical Inner Voice**

One of the surest ways to undermine feelings of confidence and inner strength is to be overly critical of ourselves. When we are in a state of fear and self-doubt, we tend to be very harsh and critical toward ourselves before, during, and after a presentation or performance. This has sometimes been referred to as the *critical parent voice* or the *inner critic*. These terms refer to that inner voice that plagues us by finding fault with ourselves, pointing out why something will not work out well, and why we are doomed to fail. Some people have grown up with a lot of criticism and lack of support and encouragement. They then go on to internalize in their own heads a similar way of speaking to themselves. Sometimes a person has created in his or her own head an almost impossible set of expectations and standards and is caught up in a vicious cycle of self-criticism, not being able to measure up to and achieve these standards. When this critical voice is activated, we find many ways to put ourselves down, to focus on our perceived weaknesses or limitations, to overlook any of our competencies or strengths, and to generally treat ourselves very harshly and unfairly. In essence, we turn against ourselves and show no compassion or support for ourselves in facing challenges and struggles. This leads us to feel even more beaten down and alone, which furthers the cycle of self-doubt and defeat.

We *must* stop this pattern of destructive self-criticism and learn to relate to ourselves in more supportive and encouraging ways, particularly when we are fearful and unsure of ourselves. This can be thought of as creating within yourself a *nurturing parent voice*, which mirrors the way a very supportive and loving parent would talk with his or her frightened child. The nurturing, loving parent would not say, "What's wrong with you? You are really going to make a fool of yourself. People are going to laugh at you. You are pathetic!"

Instead, a nurturing parent might say, "I know this is a big challenge for you and you are feeling afraid right now. It is okay to feel afraid. It doesn't mean things will go badly because you feel afraid. I know you are going to be okay, even if you don't feel that way right now. Remember, no one is expecting you to be perfect. You are great just the way you are. I believe in you! Just be who you are and do your best and that is good enough." We must create this nurturing parent voice within ourselves. We need to learn to speak to the frightened child part of ourselves with love, compassion, support, and encouragement. This childlike part of us needs more than the purely rational, reality-oriented voice of the adult perspective. It needs to hear a comforting, reassuring, encouraging softer voice that makes us feel safe and worthy to be speaking or performing in front of others.

Note the profound difference in focus, beliefs, and predictions between the critical voice and the nurturing voice. Choosing to use the nurturing voice rather than the critical voice creates a very different outcome in how we view ourselves in a public speaking or performance situation and the predictions we make about how we will do. Relating to yourself in a loving, caring manner creates deeper feelings of self-worth and safety that you carry with you into the speaking or performance event. As you create this supportive connection within yourself, you do not feel so alone and out on a limb by yourself.

It is also important that you continue this supportive inner dialogue after you have completed a speaking or performance event. Most of us tend to focus on the things that we think we did not do right or well enough, and we are disappointed and let down by our presentation or performance. Even if we have done quite well, we will focus on the one or two things we did not like, or we may focus on our upset for being so anxious in the first place. We tend to be very critical of ourselves afterward and completely overlook our abilities and strengths, as well as our courage for having presented or performed despite our fear.

Work at creating that nurturing inner voice that can validate the things you did well. Use reasonable standards rather than perfectionist ideals when you reflect on how you did in a presentation or performance. Acknowledge your abilities and your courage. Focus on the things that make you feel good about yourself rather than berate yourself for your perceived flaws. Create reasonable expectations for yourself and, if you fall short of these expectations, consider ways you can improve next time. Give yourself acknowledgment and validation for your strengths and abilities and constructive self-evaluation regarding areas of improvement. These are surefire ways to build increasing confidence for future presentations or performances. On the other hand, the combination of perfectionist or unreasonable standards and expectations, focusing on perceived shortcomings, and creating a state of disappointment and upset towards yourself are surefire ways to create even more fear and apprehension for the next time.

My personal experience with creating positive beliefs and predictions within my adult self and creating a nurturing parent voice to deal with my frightened child self have been profound. At first I did have to use the *act as if* principle because I had not had the experience upon which to build more positive beliefs and predictions about my ability to confidently handle public speaking situations. I consciously began to say things to myself that reflected positive beliefs and predictions, and I refrained from saying things that undermined my confidence and belief in myself. I took a leap of faith and kept saying these more positive and affirming things to myself even when I did not fully believe in myself. I also spoke to myself using the nurturing parent voice and was very kind and gentle with myself, creating a feeling of support and safety. I refrained from saying things to myself that created fear and self-doubt, and I began to let go of perfectionist expectations and standards. I consciously and deliberately validated my successes in mastering my fear, no matter how small or seemingly insignificant. At the same time, I also validated my growing strength and ability as a speaker, thereby creating optimistic predictions for the next time. As I took more risks to speak up, I continued to use this method to create safety and support for that child part of myself, as well as to stay as connected to adult reality as possible. This was truly a winning combination for me. It is essential that we master the art of relating to ourselves in a resourceful and empowering way in order to create the conditions for success when we present or perform in front of others.

To give you an idea of the types of things I may say to myself prior to and after giving a talk, I have included a number of them for you. Consider what works for you. What you say to yourself may change over time, depending upon your stage of development in overcoming your fear.

Things I have said to myself include:
- It is okay to feel anxious. I don't have to be afraid of my fear.
- I have to keep my focus on my purpose. I really want to help the people I am speaking to and make a difference in their lives. I need to focus on connecting with the people

in my audience.
- This is not about me.  It is about what I can offer others.
- Others are not there to scrutinize me.  They are there to learn something from me and to enjoy my presentation.
- I know I have what it takes to be a good speaker.  I just need to be who I am naturally and I will do well.
- I know my material and I know I can deliver a good presentation, even if I feel anxious.
- I know the feelings of fear don't last forever.
- Let me see myself in some situations after my talk.  I see myself driving home, having dinner, getting ready for bed.  I see myself the next day going about my routines and realizing that life goes on as normal after my presentation is over.
- Let me think about my audience and realize these are real people leading full lives.  Hearing me speak is not an earth-shattering event for these people.  I am not the center of their universe.
- Let me think back to other times I have felt successful and know that I have it in me to be successful again.
- All I need is within me right now.

Early on, I had to do a lot of nurturing inner parent talk with myself because my fear ran so deep at that time.  I would say things to my frightened child self such as:
- You are going to be okay.  Nothing bad will happen to you.  I will take care of you.
- It is okay to feel afraid.  I will be there to help you through this.  You are not alone.
- You have the right to speak up and express yourself.
- Just do your best and that is good enough.  No one is expecting perfection from you.
- The people in the audience are not monsters.  They are regular people just like you or anyone else.
- They want to hear what you think and what you have to

say.
- They respect you and like you.
- You are safe. No one is going to hurt you.
- You did a great job! I knew you could do it!

I remember a funny story of one woman I had worked with in individual counseling who was doing a lot of inner child work at the time. When she was facing a situation that was very scary and intimidating to her, she would say to that childlike part of herself, "I'll tell you what, you stay home today, and I will go out and do what I need to do. When I come home, I will let you know how it went." This really worked for her. She went off feeling and acting like a grownup and her frightened child self felt safe at home.

**SUMMARY:**
- We hold negative beliefs and create negative predictions about ourselves in a public speaking or performance situation. We tend to believe strongly in these negative thought patterns because of the intense emotional charge of the fear.
- We need to identify and confront distortions in our thinking that grossly distort our perceptions of ourselves and others when we are in public speaking or performance situations. We need to create new beliefs and predictions that are more rational and based in a more objective adult reality.
- Doing this activates our adult self and allows us to connect with our adult abilities and strengths. When we stay connected to our intense fear, we are operating more from our frightened child self, which believes in our imaginary fears just as a child believes there are m*onsters in the closet.*
- We *must* stop the *critical inner voice* that continues to undermine our confidence and belief in ourselves. Instead, we need to create a *nurturing parent voice*, which provides us

with a feeling of safety, as well as offering us support, validation, encouragement, and compassion.

- Creating feelings of safety and support for the frightened child part of ourselves, while staying as focused as possible on the objective reality perceived by our adult self, is a winning combination.

**ACTION STEPS:**

- Write a list of your negative beliefs, predictions, and thought patterns related to public speaking or performing. Carry them to whatever extreme you may go to when you feel the most panic and terror. Identify the cognitive distortions in each of these, using the list included in this chapter.
- Now write down new alternative beliefs, predictions, and thought patterns that are based in rational thinking and that reflect a more objective, adult reality. Connect with your adult self by thinking about your adult strengths and abilities.
- Work on stopping your critical inner voice related to public speaking or performing, as well as in other areas of your life. Instead, work on creating a nurturing parent voice to provide feelings of comfort and safety, as well as to support, validate, and encourage yourself. Write down things you can say to that frightened child part of you when you are facing a public speaking or performance challenge.
- Practice these new skills by creating another situation of speaking or performing in front of family and friends. Allow at least five to ten minutes for this exercise, using the same guidelines as in earlier exercises. Be sure to focus on the skills discussed in this chapter, while also using strategies learned in earlier chapters. Also to be sure to continue to update your Strategies list.
- Review these written exercises at least weekly for several months to raise your consciousness and recondition your

way of thinking and believing. Continue to review this material before a speaking or performing event in order to reinforce these new patterns of thought. Catch yourself as quickly as possible whenever you revert back to your old way of thinking, and immediately come up with a new, more resourceful way of thinking and relating to yourself.

## Chapter Eight

## *Creating A Calm And Resourceful Body And Mind*

When we perceive something as threatening or dangerous to us, our bodies have an automatic mechanism in our nervous system to protect us from potential harm. This is referred to as the fight or flight response, which was mentioned in an earlier chapter. Our body goes through a series of rapid biochemical reactions to prepare us to either fight off the perceived danger or flee the situation to get away from any potential threat or danger. Our nervous system prepares us to protect ourselves by creating an immediate arousal response that allows us to act quickly. The arousal response includes the reactions of rapid, shallow breathing; accelerated heart rate; and muscle tension. These reactions put the body in a state of readiness to ward off danger and insure our survival.

The *sympathetic nervous system* is the part of the nervous system that regulates the fight or flight response. It prepares the body to defend itself against *perceived* danger, whether it is *real* or *imagined*. For example, this arousal system can become triggered just as strongly by the real danger of having a stranger chase you down a dark alley as by the imagined danger of having to speak or perform in front of an audience. If your mind perceives something to be a significant danger or threat to your well-being, and inputs this perception to your nervous system, it will act upon the input without evaluating the actual reality of the threat. It will immediately respond with arousal of the body without questioning the realness of the threat. So it is up to us to perceive situations more accurately and to distinguish between real and imagined threats so as not to give our nervous system false cues. I used to feel as though my body was betraying me by being so out of control with surges of intense physical sensations. I now have come to understand that my body was doing exactly what it was supposed to do based on my perceptions of threat and danger. My sympathetic nervous system was attempting to protect my survival, but was not able to distinguish that this was an imagined danger rather than a real danger.

The *parasympathetic nervous system* is the part of the nervous system that serves to calm and slow down the arousal of the body when the perception of significant threat or danger is no longer there. This part of our nervous system brings our body back into balance after arousal has taken place and we are no longer feeling threatened. These two parts of the nervous system work together in a complementary way, with one or the other part being dominant at any given time. While they function in an automatic, involuntary manner, they are also subject to being influenced by conscious, deliberate behavior. This is especially important to realize because it gives us an inroad to controlling our inner physical reactions. This is achieved through a combination of changing our perceptions so that we do not input false cues signaling danger and by using other methods to bring about a relaxation response in the body.

**Shifting Perceptions**

In the area of changing perceptions, we need to focus on, think about, and say things to ourselves that create more feelings of safety and trust in ourselves and others. Instead of fueling all of our imaginary fears and doom and gloom predictions, we need to be grounded in our adult selves as much as possible. We need to more accurately assess the reality of the situation and our capacity to handle the demands of the situation in our adult role. My perceptions of a public speaking or performance situation have dramatically changed as I have done the work to overcome my fear. I am now able to perceive the situation more realistically from my adult self rather than from distorted perceptions which arise out of a more regressed, childlike mind-set. For example, I will share with you some of my earlier distorted perceptions that created my inner terror and mistrust, and my current perceptions that now create feelings of trust and safety.

### *My Earlier Perceptions:*
- I thought people were looking for what was wrong with me and judging my worth as a person.
- I felt so alone and out on a limb all by myself with no support.
- I thought people would lose respect for me and pity me if they saw how anxious I was.
- I felt as though people could see through me and see that I was not as confident as I tried to portray myself to the world.
- I perceived people in the audience as though they were monsters, ready to pounce on me if I did anything wrong.
- I felt it was me against them, and I could not let them see me afraid or they would take advantage of that.
- I experienced the situation as though I was on trial and facing a possible death sentence whenever I had to give a presentation.
- I felt I could not trust myself because of feeling so out of control in my mind and my body.
- I felt like a little child put in front of a group of grownups.

I was expected to pull it off and act like a grownup, without anyone detecting how I really felt.

- I felt I could never be the real me. I thought it wasn't safe, and that I might get hurt if I let my guard down.

*My Current Perceptions:*
- My purpose in speaking is to contribute to others and make a difference in their lives with whatever information or insight I can offer.
- The people in the audience are real people just like me. I need to focus on connecting with each of them as individuals and creating a feeling of warmth and welcoming toward them.
- This is not about me. The audience is not here to scrutinize me and assess my worth as a person. People are coming to hear me speak to see if they can get something of value for themselves.
- I want to give lovingly and generously to my audience. I want to really help others by what I share and express.
- I believe that I have all of the resources within me to do a good job. I trust in myself and in divine guidance that I will be able to give something of value to my audience.
- It is okay to be who I really am. I am not here to impress people or to gain their approval. I am here to give to others, and I can do this best when I am being who I really am rather than trying to be someone I am not.
- It is okay if I feel some anxiety as I prepare to speak. This is normal and natural. I know I can function well even if I feel anxious.
- I know I will feel less anxious as I focus on giving to the audience and forget about myself.
- I want to have fun with my audience. I want to lighten up the atmosphere and make people feel good to be here.

As you can see, there is a huge contrast between my old perceptions and my current ones.  My earlier perceptions quickly produced a fight or flight response to protect my survival as my mind perceived an imagined danger.  At that time I did not understand what was happening in my body, so my body's response became even more of a threat to me as I perceived myself completely out of control and having no escape. My mind and body's reactions fueled a very negative feedback loop that escalated into a full-blown panic attack on many occasions.  This set the stage for me to brace myself for the next time, predicting I would end up going through a similar traumatic reaction each time I had to speak.  These reactions and predictions stacked on each other to create an ever-increasing perception of threat and danger whenever I had to speak in front of others.

My current perceptions are vastly different in focus and lead to a feeling of trust and safety rather than a state of alarm and danger.  These perceptions do not trigger a fight or flight response because I am no longer creating imagined danger in my mind.  As my perceptions have become more reality oriented and adult like, my feelings of safety and trust have continued to increase.  As I have started to perceive more safety, my parasympathetic nervous system is more dominant and creates a calming response in my body.  This response further reinforces feelings of safety as I no longer experience my body as being so out of control.  So, at last, my mind and body are now working together to create more of a state of calm rather than a state of terror!  This has allowed me to build more trust and confidence in myself, and my predictions about future times of speaking in front of others has become more positive and encouraging.

Shifting my beliefs and perceptions in this way did not happen overnight.  It was a process, like most things, of letting go of the old and letting in the new.  Sometimes I had to act as if I had these more resourceful beliefs and perceptions when I felt more shaky. This always helped, at least to some extent, as it allowed me to try on a set of new beliefs and perceptions that were more resourceful. It also allowed me to recondition myself in adopting a new way of thinking. After some time of doing this, I started to build up positive experiences of feeling more calm and confident, and I used these as reference experiences to create more positive expectations for future speaking situations. I had finally stepped out of the vicious cycle I had been in and stepped into a positive and empowering feedback loop.

**Creating Humor**

I have also used other strategies and techniques to shift my beliefs and perceptions and to calm my nervous system. In addition to strategies discussed in earlier chapters, I will mention a number of other things I have done, and have taught others to do, which have been useful.

One technique is sometimes referred to as a *scrambling technique,* which has been adapted from the discipline of *Neurolinguistic Programming (NLP).* I encourage you to read more about NLP as it offers a range of techniques to help you make shifts in your perceptions of a situation or experience as well as some specific exercises to deal with phobias. In the scrambling technique, you first imagine in your mind, as vividly as possible using all of your senses, the experience of your worst fear in a public speaking or performance situation. Once you have that clearly in mind, you then begin to scramble images around in your mind and make the picture as ridiculous, silly, and bizarre as you possibly can. You can make people have wings flying around the room, you can put yourself on stilts or stand on your head looking at everyone upside down, you can see people turning different colors and wearing pink polka dot dresses and suits, or whatever your creative imagination will allow. You will likely find yourself giggling at the silly images you create in your mind. As soon as you think you have created the most silly image you can imagine, make it even more silly and bizarre.

The point of this exercise is that you are scrambling the image so much that you can not even distinguish it as the same original scary image anymore. It is helpful to reinforce this new association by creating a vivid picture of your silly scenario in your mind until you find it easily accessed whenever you start to become afraid. Then, whenever your mind starts to think of the worst case scenarios, it will immediately associate to your silly, stupid, bizarre image, and you will start to chuckle to yourself. You are also free to create new and different silly images to keep it as novel and interesting as possible.

Before reading further, I would like you to take a minute to try this first technique. Read over the directions first, then put the book down and try this while it is fresh in mind. I urge you to do these exercises when I suggest, rather than wait, because it helps to immediately experience each of these techniques after they are fully described. You will be better able to learn and remember the techniques if you take the time to try each one out fully.

- First, using all of your senses (seeing, hearing, feeling, tasting, and smelling), create a vivid image of yourself in your worst case speaking or performance situation messing up in the worst way. Hold that image a moment until it is clearly in mind.
- Then, start to reshape the image into the most bizarre and ridiculous image you can possibly imagine. Unleash that playful child part of yourself and let your imagination go wild! Be as silly as you possibly can, and then go one step beyond and make it even sillier! Have fun with this and allow yourself to enjoy your creation.
- Now, go back to the original doom and gloom image, and immediately scramble it back to the silly image. Repeat this procedure five times until the association becomes linked. Note your own reactions to this exercise. Imagine

yourself in the real situation thinking of this and chuckling quietly to yourself about your own inside joke.

In follow-up contacts with class participants, a number of people have reported using this technique very successfully when they have had to give a presentation or performance. The humor immediately stopped them from getting into an overly serious, doom and gloom mind-set and created a spirit of lightness and fun. They found themselves with a smile on their faces rather than a furrow on their brows, and this further reinforced a positive outlook and disposition.

**Creating Confidence**

Another technique that is immensely helpful is referred to as *positive visualization* or *mental imagery*. You may have heard of this technique used in sports psychology and success coaching. It has been shown to be very effective, both in creating high levels of confidence and in actually improving performance. This fits with the model of the self-fulfilling prophesy, which states that what we focus on and believe about ourselves tends to come true. So, if we focus on negative images and predictions, we set ourselves up for dramatically reduced confidence and lower performance levels. On the other hand, if we focus on and create resourceful images and thoughts, we create an internal state of confidence and positive predictions. This state leads to higher levels of performance and reinforces further confidence and future success. In the sports arena, a player may see himself or herself playing a game successfully over and over in his or her mind's eye before actually getting onto the field or court. The player anticipates how he or she will play the game, play by play, easily scoring, easily recovering from any difficult plays, with great confidence and success. The player sees himself or herself celebrating success at completion of the game and hearing cheers from the crowds. The player replays these images of success over and over, steadily

gaining confidence and creating a peak state, which then car-
ries over to the actual performance. We can use the same basic
principle in preparing ourselves mentally prior to a speaking
or performance event. Up until now, we have set ourselves up
to feel demoralized, self-doubting, and insecure by our negative focus and predictions. It is not surprising that we have
arrived at a speaking or performance event feeling shaky and
helpless, because we have created this disempowered state
through our negative mental preparation. Our performance
has also likely suffered to some degree as a result of a negative
self-fulfilling prophesy.

We must change our strategy in anticipation of a speaking
or performance event. It is important to mentally prepare ourselves in a way that creates confidence and a peak mental state.
We must anticipate and prepare for success, not failure. We
need to image ourselves feeling confident; being in a peak state
while presenting or performing, sometimes referred to as being
"in the flow," where everything flows naturally and effortless-
ly; easily and effectively responding to any challenges that
come up; and celebrating our success with hearing the
applause, feeling proud of our ourselves and our accomplishment.

It may be hard at first to see yourself as confident and
successful if you are so used to doubting yourself and feeling
like a failure. You may have to act as if you are feeling confident about your ability to be successful before you develop the
actual feelings of confidence and trust in yourself. Even if the
feelings are not completely genuine at this time, it is still very
useful to do this exercise over and over to begin to recondition
yourself for success. Many highly successful people in other
walks of life regularly think this way, and this has been a very
large part of their success. Before these people actually became
successful, they first created their success in their minds. It is
said that what is created first in the mind ultimately becomes
manifested in the external reality. We can use this principle to

recondition our minds with a regular focus on positive, empowering images and thoughts. We must take our focus off of our fear and focus instead on our desired outcomes.

Some people have shared that they are afraid to do this because they may disappoint themselves if they do not achieve success, and they may not be prepared if something bad happens. This type of thinking is self-defeating. It focuses on the possibility that something bad might happen rather than focusing on the high probability that good things will happen with positive mental preparation. If you are thinking this way, I urge you to challenge the distortions in your belief system and give yourself a chance to create a more empowering way of thinking. I have used this principle very successfully in the area of public speaking, as well as in other areas of my life. I do not usually go frame by frame in mentally imaging my success in a speaking event as some people do. Instead, I create an overall image of entering and moving through the speaking event with confidence, effectiveness, and ease. I feel the confidence as I create this empowering image and reinforce it with affirming thoughts and a positive focus on my purpose. I image myself feeling deeply connected to my audience and enjoying the process of sharing with them what I have to say. I image myself at the end feeling proud of my accomplishment and seeing people in my audience acknowledging me for the positive impact I have made in their lives. As I review this a number of times before a speaking event, I feel even more confident that I can accomplish my purpose when the actual speaking event takes place. In my imagery, it is not about me being a superstar and basking in the applause. Rather, it is about me being a confident and effective speaker who is able to achieve her purpose to positively affect her audience and make a real difference in their lives.

Now, I would like you to try this positive visualization exercise for yourself. Be sure to adapt it to your own speaking or performing circumstances. First read the directions for the exercise, and then put the book down and try it out.

- Using all of your senses, vividly imagine yourself first hearing about a presentation or performance you are being asked to give. Immediately start to feel very open and welcoming of the opportunity. Start to feel the trust and belief in yourself, knowing you will be able to do this well.

- Then image yourself in the days, weeks, or months prior to the presentation or performance, feeling calm and relaxed about the upcoming event, confident in your ability to do well.

- See yourself preparing for the presentation or performance, feeling very good about your ability to deliver it in a powerful and effective manner.

- See yourself the day before the event continuing to feel confident and calm. It is the night before the event and you are having a restful night's sleep and feeling very refreshed and positive the morning of the event.

- Image yourself on the way over to the event, feeling a deep sense of confident, positive expectation of your ability to do well.

- Start to imagine the presentation or performance itself, vividly imaging yourself moving through this event with ease and effectiveness, enjoying the feeling of being in the flow.

- See yourself easily and comfortably handling any challenges that come up. You are clear in your thinking and focused on your purpose.

- Imagine being deeply connected to your audience and enjoying the process of speaking or performing. See yourself feeling a proud sense of accomplishment as your audience acknowledges the positive impact you have made in their lives.

- Walk away from the event holding on to the good feelings and feeling full confidence in your abilities as a speaker or performer to contribute powerfully to the lives of others.

Create an image of yourself looking forward to future opportunities to speak or perform again.

While this visualization may feel light years away from how you see yourself right now, it is essential that you start to create a new image of yourself as a speaker or performer. This technique is one of the most effective ways to do so. The field of *psychocybernetics* refers to this as mental rehearsal in the *theater of your mind*. We must come to redefine our self-image and see ourselves as capable of experiencing public speaking and performance with confidence, ease, joy, and success. I urge you to use this technique regularly to recondition your mind and to see a whole new possibility for yourself that you never imagined possible!

**Expanding Your Identity**

I have also used the principle of *role modeling* to expand my image of myself related to speaking in public. This principle is also used in the area of success coaching and peak performance training. The idea behind this principle is that you can adopt new behaviors or personal qualities by actively modeling yourself after someone who has the behaviors or qualities that you desire for yourself. I regularly read about and hear about people who are top performers in speaking, performing, and other walks of life. I listen carefully for the operating principles by which they live their lives and the principles that make them so successful. I then consider how I might be able to apply these principles in my own life. Doing this has accelerated my learning curve and has given me some guidelines to live my life by that have contributed to an increase in my effectiveness and success.

While I use these principles in all areas of my life, I especially look for ways I can apply them in the area of public speaking and performing. Some of the core operating principles I have learned and actively use in the process of role modeling others include:

- Have a mission and purpose larger than yourself when you speak or perform in front of others. You must have a strong desire to make a difference in the lives of others.

- Keep your focus on making a strong and deep connection with your audience. This is how you can create the most impact on others and effectively achieve your purpose. Experiencing and expressing love and connection eliminate fear.

- Your purpose is not to gain the approval of others, but to add value to the lives of others.

- Prepare yourself by creating a positive mind-set and positive expectation before you speak or perform. Reference in your mind other times when you have been at peak performance in your life, and connect with the state you were in at that time. Know that you can recreate that state again as you go into any new situation of speaking or performing.

- Create a peak physical state in your body by doing things that create a feeling of relaxed energy, alertness, and strength in your physical body.

- See each situation of speaking or performing as a golden opportunity to grow beyond your own perceived limitations and to make a larger impact in the world.

- We grow most when we are outside of our comfort zones and take the risk to enter the area of the unknown. Look for the lessons each time you are in uncertain territory and feeling uncomfortable.

- It is okay to make mistakes or to experience rejection. It does not mean you are a failure. Most successful people have made many mistakes and have experienced rejection numerous times. These experiences did not defeat them or lead them to lose faith in themselves. Rather, they focused on the lessons to be learned and moved on, resolved in their determination to succeed.

- Always have faith and trust that you have all that you need within you to be successful. You can tap into that power within you by believing in yourself and in a higher power who guides you.
- Focus on and celebrate your successes and achievements. Expect the best from yourself and you will get the best.

These are some of the basic principles I use to guide my life. I find that when I also use these principles to empower myself in other areas of my life, I have more faith and trust in myself when it comes to speaking in front of others. I am now aware that I am responsible for actively creating my state of mind and body to be confident and strong. I give as much priority to preparing my mind and body with *the right psychology* and *the right physiology* for peak performance as I do to preparing the material I will be presenting to the audience. I used to think that if I did not have the natural ability to speak with confidence and ease in front of others, I was doomed to be afraid forever. I have discovered this is not so. I have learned to do things that create my own belief and trust in myself and allow me to be the best of who I am in front of others.

### Positive Self-Care

In addition to creating a positive focus in my mind and talking to myself in language that creates trust and confidence in myself, I also do other things to generate a positive state. I value a healthy lifestyle and good self-care, which lead me to feel at my best and be at my best. I regularly follow a health-conscious vegetarian diet, drink plenty of water, drink no caffeinated beverages, and exercise routinely. While you may not choose to embrace this type of lifestyle, I strongly encourage you to stay away from caffeine, eat a healthy diet, and exercise moderately for several days before a presentation or performance.

It is also good to do other things to promote healthy self-care and create relaxation, especially prior to a presentation or performance. For me this might include things like getting a massage, doing yoga, reading, taking baths, resting and getting enough sleep, and finding things that make me smile and laugh.

I also like to listen to music and have certain CD's and tapes that I have come to associate with feelings of strength, power, and joy. I regularly listen to that music several days before I am to present, as well as when I am on my way to the presentation. For me, certain music has become an anchor to help me easily access my inner feelings of strength, confidence, and belief in myself. It is important to find the things that create for you peak states of relaxation, positive energy, and confidence and to actively do those things prior to presenting or performing.

It is especially important to stay away from things that create lethargy, self-doubt, and agitation prior to presenting or performing. These include eating junk food or skipping meals, drinking coffee, procrastinating, rushing around, and staying up late to complete your preparation. These types of behaviors increase tension, stress, and fatigue and make it that much harder to create a peak state of mind and body.

### Creating A Relaxed And Resourceful Body

You can also do some specific exercises to create a relaxed state in your mind and body. There are two specific relaxation exercises I will describe for this purpose. Some people may also want to look into learning about meditation, as this can be a very effective practice to calm and center the mind and body. While doing these exercises, you may want to play calming and soothing music, if it helps you to relax.

### *Progressive Relaxation Method*

The first exercise is a version of the *Progressive Relaxation* method, developed by Edmund Jacobson. It is a classic relaxation exercise used effectively by many people. The best way to practice this exercise is to go to a quiet place where you can lie down and not be disturbed.

- Start by focusing awareness on your breath. Try to clear your mind and keep your focus on your breath. Start to do some deep breathing to center yourself and begin the process of relaxation.

- Now focus your attention on your feet and toes. Create muscle tension in your feet and toes and feel the tension. Hold the tension for a few seconds, and then gently and gradually let go and release the tension, until it all fades away.

- Move your attention up to your calves and thighs. Create tension in this area of your body. Hold the tension. Feel the tension. Let go and release the tension from this part of your body, letting the tension dissolve out into the air around you until it evaporates.

- Continue to do the same process in each area as you move up through your body, going next to your buttocks, your lower back, your upper back, your shoulders and neck, your stomach area, your upper chest, your arms, your hands and fingers, your mouth and jaw, your nose, cheeks and temples, your eyes and forehead, and your scalp.

- After you have created tension, held the tension, and released the tension in each area of your body, then create tension in your whole body. Hold this tension, feel it, and with a long, deep sigh, release the tension throughout your whole body and feel it dissipate into nothingness in the air around you.

- You may also want to envision a stream of relaxing, healing energy flowing through you from the top of your head throughout all the organs, muscles, and cells in your body, cleansing and healing your body in the process. See any residue of tension or stress being carried away by the stream as it moves down through your body and is released through your feet and toes.

If possible, stop reading and try this method for ten to fifteen minutes before reading about the next exercise. If not, be sure you come back to this exercise as soon as possible and try it.

### *The Autogenic Training Method*

Another type of relaxation exercise is like a form of self-hypnosis and is called *The Autogenic Training Method*. Using this method, you will make the following suggestions to different parts of your body: "My _____ feels heavy, limp, loose, and relaxed."

- It is best to start at your head and work your way downward, thinking quietly and slowly to yourself, "My head feels heavy, limp, loose, and relaxed." Hold the feeling, then go on to the next area in your body.

- "My neck and shoulders feel heavy, limp, loose, and relaxed." Hold the feeling, then move on with "My upper back feels heavy, limp, loose, and relaxed."

- Continue with this process as you suggest this to your lower back, your upper chest, your arms, your hands and fingers, your stomach area, your buttocks, your thighs and calves, and your feet and toes. Hold the relaxation in each area of your body before moving to the next area.

- Then suggest to your whole body, "My whole body feels heavy, limp, loose, and relaxed" and experience this sensation throughout your body.

- The feeling you are aiming to create is one of being a rag doll with no muscle tension or strain. You can substitute other words for the ones in this suggestion if you find other words more effective for creating deep relaxation in your body.

If possible, stop reading further and try this second relaxation exercise now. If not, be sure to try this as soon as you can. Focus on the suggestions and see how you feel with this relaxation exercise, compared to *Progressive Relaxation*.

Some people find it hard to do these exercises without being verbally guided. If that is the case for you, you may want to read the instructions into a tape recorder. Or you may want to purchase a relaxation tape. Many people prefer one of these exercises over the other. Some people like both equally and some people do not respond particularly well to either one. Notice what your preferences are and what works best for you. You can adapt these exercises to work for you, or create a different exercise of your own making to create a state of relaxation. You decide. You may also use an abbreviated version of these exercises whenever you need them by simply focusing in on one or a few areas in the body that are feeling tense and in need of relaxation. Remember, muscle tension is part of the fight or flight response, and it is helpful to have a method to release this tension from the body in order to give your nervous system feedback that you are safe and there is no need to prepare your body for a survival response.

**Expressing Emotional States**

Another aspect of the body that is helpful to pay attention to is how your body expresses your emotional states. When you are experiencing feelings of fear, anxiety, tension, worry, and self-doubt your body has a certain posture and way of expressing these emotions. Usually you can feel your body constrict inward and become stiff and rigid. You may also find yourself holding your head low with your eyes focused downward. You may find yourself with a furrowed brow and tension in certain parts of your body. Take a moment right now and recreate the body posture and facial expressions that your body normally assumes when you feel fear, anxiety, tension, and self-doubt prior to speaking or performing. Try this sitting down, standing up, and walking around the room. Observe how your body expresses these emotions.

Now imagine the highest level of fear you have felt with speaking or performing, perhaps a state of panic and dread, and experience how your body expresses this intense emotional state. Again, try this sitting, standing, and walking around. Notice how your body expresses this heightened emotional state. Relax your body and shake out all of the tension and stiffness your body has just experienced.

Now, by contrast, assume the body posture and facial expressions that you normally would have when you are in a peak state. Imagine feeling the best you can possibly feel, experiencing a calm, relaxed, and centered state. Imagine feelings of incredible confidence and self-assurance, of trust in yourself and the world around you. Imagine being in a totally empowered state, a feeling of being in the flow. Reconnect with a memory of a time you felt like this. If you have not felt this great at some time in your life, imagine what it would be like. Create and enjoy the expression of these feelings in your body. Feel your vital life energy being freely expressed throughout your body. Observe the contrast in your body when you are in a peak emotional state as compared to being in a fearful and self-doubting emotional state.

As we discussed earlier, your mind and body are interconnected and strongly influence each other. When you are in a certain emotional state, it will be reflected in your body. And when you are assuming certain facial expressions and body posture, they will provide feedback to your mind. While this process is generally automatic and something that we normally do not pay attention to, we can actually influence our feeling state by consciously and deliberately assuming certain facial expressions and body postures.

I would like you to practice creating facial expressions and body postures that reflect confidence, self-assurance, relaxation, and positive life energy over the coming week. Create this experience in your body while sitting down, standing up, and walking around. Chances are your head is held high, your eyes look upward and take in a broad view, your chest is out, your shoulders are back, your back is straight but not rigid, your muscles are firm but flexible, a smile is on your face, your gait is strong and directed. When you make this process conscious, it is yet another way that you can influence the creation of a more positive emotional state.

You can consciously and deliberately adopt facial expressions and a body posture congruent with a positive, calm, and confident emotional state. Be aware of any gestures you now make that undermine this empowered state. I remember a woman in one of my classes who had a particularly noticeable facial and body expression that showed alarm and panic anytime she heard she had to give a talk. You can imagine that this alarmed body gesture reinforced her perception of threat and danger and added further feedback to her nervous system that fueled the fight or flight response.

Try to detect if you have any obvious pattern of facial and body expressions that express fear and worry. You may want to ask someone close to you for input on this as it is often hard to see ourselves objectively. If you have any detectable pattern of negative response in your body, be sure to consciously and deliberately work to eliminate this pattern so it frees you to adopt more resourceful facial expressions and body posture.

### Creating Resourceful Language

Another expression of our emotional state is seen in our use of language and how we express ourselves verbally. Similar to how our bodies express our emotions, our language both expresses and reinforces a certain emotional state. When we are feeling fear, worry, and self-doubt, we express ourselves differently than when we are feeling relaxed, trusting, and self-assured.

Just as with our body language, we are often unaware that how we are expressing ourselves verbally is actually reinforcing and fueling our fearful, self-doubting emotional state. For example, when having to speak or perform in front of others, it is not uncommon to hear things like "Oh no, I can't do this."

"Maybe I can get out of this one." "I can't wait until this is over." We often say things like this, and sometimes things far worse, without thinking.

Each time we do, we further reinforce our fear and self-doubt. We need to be more conscious of the language we are using to express ourselves verbally, and to consciously and deliberately adopt a more empowering vocabulary. Instead of feeding our fear, we need to choose language that nourishes a feeling of trust, calm, and confidence. Even if we do not feel these positive emotions, we need to act as if and say things that support a more positive and empowered emotional state. We need to express ourselves more calmly and confidently as we face a speaking or performing situation. We can say things like, "Yes, I would be happy to accept this speaking (or performing) opportunity. Thank you!" "I look forward to getting the chance to speak (or perform) for your group." "I am sure things will go very well."

Whether we are speaking to someone else, or to ourselves, we need to stay positive and strong in our language. When we do this in both our verbal and nonverbal communication, it builds our emotional strength.

Now, reflect a moment on how you express yourself verbally when you are in a state of fear and self-doubt. Note the things you say, and how saying these things further reinforce a loss of trust and belief in yourself. Practice saying something different instead. Say things that support a feeling of calm, trust, confidence, and strength that you want to create for yourself. Don't worry if you do not believe in what you say at first. It takes time to recondition your emotional state, just as it takes time to build muscle when you start to work out. To build muscle emotionally, we need to regularly reinforce a positive mental state as much as possible. In the meantime, before you more fully believe in yourself, act as if you believe in yourself and express this in more positive and empowering language.

**SUMMARY:**

- The fight or flight response is our body's natural mechanism to protect us from harm and is triggered by our perception of danger, whether that danger is *real* or *imagined*. Our perception of psychological threat or danger in public speaking or performing is enough to trigger a fight or flight response, which leads to the physical symptoms that make us feel such a loss of control.

- We must work toward shifting our perceptions of public speaking or performing so we do not interpret it as an unsafe situation. When we stop imagining serious threat and danger, the fight or flight response is no longer triggered, and we begin to feel in control of ourselves.

- You can use various techniques to change your perceptions of public speaking or performing, including a *scrambling technique* to perceive the situation with humor and a *visualization technique* to create positive mental imagery about speaking or performing in public.

- It is also very helpful to identify with role models who demonstrate more resourceful states related to public speaking or performing. Identifying with positive role models can help you to expand your own identity and to create peak performance in many areas of your life.

- It is very important to engage in good self-care, particularly prior to giving a presentation or performance. Eliminate caffeine from your diet, strive to eat healthy foods, exercise moderately, do things that create relaxation and enjoyment, and get plenty of sleep and rest.

- Consider using relaxation exercises to reduce muscle tension and to relax your mind and body. You can also do an abbreviated version of these exercises to release tension in particular areas of your body.

- Pay attention to the physiology in your body - your body posture and facial expressions can reinforce your emotional state. Adopt a physiology that supports a calm and confident state of mind.

- Pay attention to the language you use to express yourself - this can also reinforce your emotional state. Use resourceful language that reinforces feelings of safety, trust, and belief in yourself. Act as if you believe in yourself if you are not quite there yet.

**ACTION STEPS:**

- Imagine you are a world-renowned expert in creating a state of fear, terror, dread, self-doubt, and mistrust in yourself and others when it comes to public speaking or performing. Further imagine you have been hired as a consultant to share your secret method for creating a state of inner panic and terror. Write down a very detailed step by step procedure to follow so that anyone could duplicate your fool-proof method for creating such inner terror. Be sure to include things you think and say to yourself, your beliefs and perceptions about imagined threat and danger, what dire things you predict will happen to you, what you do prior to a presentation or performance to work yourself up and to create tremendous self-doubt and mistrust, and what you do in your body to create tension and further reinforce a feeling of helplessness and loss of control. Have fun with this *Recipe for Disaster* exercise as you come to appreciate the inevitable outcome of panic and terror, based on how you approach the situation.

- Now imagine that you are no longer an expert at creating panic and terror and that you have fully overcome your fear of public speaking or performing. You have now become a world-renowned expert at creating a calm and confident state of mind and body. Further imagine you have been hired as a consultant to teach others your proven methods for success in this area. Using what you have learned thus far, write down a step by step procedure that is a surefire way to create feelings of calm and resourcefulness in your mind and body, belief and trust in yourself and others, positive expectancy, and high levels of self-assurance and self-confidence. Have fun with this exercise, too, recognizing you now have the foundation you need to create a resourceful and empowered state of mind and body to face any public speaking or performing situation. Keep this *Recipe for Success* visible and review it daily over the next ten days and frequently thereafter. Reviewing it regularly will help to accelerate your learning curve and recondition your way of thinking and responding to any public speaking or performing situation.

- Do further hands-on practice of speaking or performing, with the focus on applying strategies learned in this chapter and reinforcement of methods learned in earlier chapters. Create a situation where you will be able to speak or perform in front of a group of family and friends for at least ten to fifteen minutes for practice and support, using the same guidelines as in earlier speaking or performing exercises. Remember to update your Strategies List to use as a reference for the many things you have available to you to reduce your experience of fear and to increase your feelings of confidence and control.

## Chapter Nine

### *Getting To The Source*

We all carry emotional baggage with us, whether it relates to our family background, our early experience with teachers and peers, or our experience in our teenage and early adult years. We may have had some earlier painful life experiences that have not been fully resolved within ourselves. The earlier pain may relate to one or more traumatic events in our lives or it may be associated with more subtle pain, such as the pain of receiving ongoing or harsh criticism, judgment, discipline, disapproval, ridicule, lack of support and encouragement, or having very high expectations placed on you and never feeling you were good enough.

These earlier life events play a part in shaping the person you become and they affect your self-image and your perception of others. The deeper pain we have experienced related to life events in our past may not be on our minds consciously, but it can be projected onto something in our present lives and reflected in a current personal struggle. In the case of our fear of speaking or performing in front of others, there is a deeper source to our fear and mistrust of ourselves and others. There is also a deeper source to our feeling such a lack of safety in being who we really are in front of others.

In my own life I had several traumatic experiences that led me to feel a lack of safety and support as a child. When I was seven years old my mother died, which left a tremendous void in my family. I remember feeling very alone and without support. Following her death, there was a lot of chaos in my family. My father remarried, and there was ongoing conflict and turmoil in our home for years. My father and stepmother divorced after five years of major turmoil and there was further disruption in the family related to the process of divorce. I never paid too much attention to my feelings about all of this and tried to stay busy and leave this all behind me.

As I tried to better understand the source of my fear of public speaking, I became aware of how my feelings of fear and lack of safety and support from my past was becoming displaced onto the current situation of speaking in front of others. I became aware of how I was unconsciously projecting feelings from my past onto the present situation, which was leading me to feel a similar loss of control that I felt as a child. Specifically, in the speaking situation, I came to perceive myself as out on a limb, all by myself without support, as I had felt as a child. I came to be very afraid of the silence of the audience with all their eyes on me. I associated this with feeling the tension in my home when the silent treatment was going on, as I knew something bad was brewing or had just happened. I used to do my best to hide out so I would not be the target of anger and rage. I would be waiting for the shoe to drop, anxiously anticipating something awful was going to happen, which it generally did. My biggest chance at surviving was to be a good girl and stay out of harm's way.

In the public speaking situation, I projected a similar power onto the audience as my family life once had had over me. I experienced the same helplessness and loss of control with the audience as I did with my family. I felt the same mistrust and lack of safety with the audience as I did within my family life. I had the same need to be a good girl by striving for perfection so that no one could find any fault with me and turn against me. I felt that same need to please so that I would stay on the good side of those who could harm me. In short, every time I went into a public speaking situation it was as though I was that little girl reliving my threatening family life over again. This was all very unconscious, and I had never understood the connection until a few years ago when I did some deeper exploration of the origin of my fear. When I was able to see how I was reexperiencing my earlier unresolved feelings of fear and pain from my past, I was able to work more on dealing with the original source of my pain and separate it from my present experience. I saw a therapist to address the earlier issues from my life more directly so I could deal with the deeper source of my fear and mistrust. This effort helped me to be able to perceive the public speaking situation more accurately and realistically from my adult self because I was no longer so triggered by frightening associations from my past.

**Understanding The Source Of Our Fear**

In my classes, we do a writing exercise to help class participants get to the source of their fear of public speaking or performing. Some people have chosen to share with me the origin of their fear. While some have had more traumatic life events, especially within their family background, others have had more subtle pain associated with harsh or ongoing criticism from parents, parents who were overly strict or controlling, parents who were judgmental and had high expectations that could never be satisfied, or parents who were discouraging and unsupportive.

Other people have had a generally supportive family but have experienced embarrassing ridicule from a teacher or peers. There may have been one particularly painful experience from the past or there may have been a number of instances of feeling a lack of caring and support from significant others.

The point of getting to the source of our fear is not to blame our parents, teachers, or peers for our problem. Rather, it is to better understand ourselves and to stop blaming ourselves for having this problem. The point is to blame no one. Instead, the focus is on better understanding the circumstances of our own particular life history that led to our vulnerability to developing this type of problem.

In reflecting back on our past, it is helpful to consider times in our earlier life when we have felt a loss of control; when we may have felt helpless and powerless; embarrassed, inadequate, and incompetent; ashamed of ourselves or our families; different from everyone else; unsafe and not able to trust others; disapproved of and not accepted; or not good enough.

Many times, because of our earlier life experience, we have come to feel ashamed of ourselves and our vulnerability. We feel as though we are different, that we are defective in some way, that there is something wrong with us. We often try to cover up these feelings, afraid that others will be able to see through us and see all of our perceived inadequacies. In my own background, I grew up feeling very different because of not having a mother and having such a chaotic family life. I felt ashamed of my family and of myself. I did not want anyone to know how bad it was in my home because I felt as though it was a reflection on me. I felt there was something wrong with me because there was something wrong with my family. I never wanted to reveal too much about myself because I felt I would be judged poorly.

I generally felt comfortable interacting with people one-on-one or casually in small groups because I felt I had more control over these interactions and could gauge peoples' responses to me. I never felt comfortable being in front of larger groups in formal settings, however, as I felt I could not control these interactions. I was very afraid of the visibility of being in front of others. It felt as though I was on display for all to look at and judge. I felt as though I was transparent and that things would be revealed about me that I did not want people to see. I was especially fearful that the audience would see how afraid I was and think there was something really wrong with me. The silence of the group, with all of their eyes on me, made me feel as though I was being watched closely and that others may not see me as strong and as capable as I wanted to appear. I was ashamed of not feeling strong in front of others, and I was afraid they would either take advantage of my vulnerability or pity me.

I have heard of some people who are more comfortable with larger groups and more threatened by one-on-one or small group interactions. In talking with these people, it is interesting to see that the reverse is true for them. They are more afraid of being seen too closely and judged poorly when they are in one-on-one or small group interactions. They are less afraid in front of larger groups because they feel they can hide their true selves more easily in front of a larger, more anonymous group.

While the threat shows itself differently, it is still the same fear of not having control over what others think about us. It reflects the same deeper shame around feeling we are not good enough and the fear that others will discover this about us. As I had mentioned in an earlier chapter, this feeling can coincide with a basically good self-esteem, at least when we are operating within our comfort zones and feel control over ourselves and our activities. When we step outside of this comfort zone, however, our self-esteem is tested most and feelings of self-doubt and inadequacy can show themselves. This was true for me. I generally felt capable and competent in most areas of my life, but when I was exposed to the view of an audience I lost touch with my self-assuredness and experienced myself as weak and vulnerable, which took a toll on my self-esteem.

While some people have had a lifelong fear of speaking or performing in public, other people have developed this fear after years of feeling relatively comfortable in this arena.

Especially for the latter group of people, it is helpful to explore circumstances in your current life and recent past for clues as to what might have triggered this fear at this time in your life. It may be that particular stresses led this fear to surface now in your life. While current stresses may have triggered this fear, it is also helpful to explore your past history for earlier painful experiences that may have set the stage for developing this type of problem.

You may have already given some thought to the origins of your fear of public speaking or performing, or this may be a new exploration for you. While insight is helpful, insight alone rarely shifts your emotional experience. It is more helpful if you can connect emotionally with your earlier life experience and feel the pain that you felt then, with deep empathy for yourself. It is healing when you can be with that pain and nurture yourself through it with a caring and compassionate attitude toward yourself. It is important to get to the source of your fear and mistrust of yourself and others, your shame and your feeling of not being good enough, your fear of being seen and being heard, and your belief that people will judge you harshly and not accept you as you are.

As with most things, it makes sense to deal with the root of the problem rather than only trying to remedy the symptoms. If this seems too overwhelming to do on your own, I recommend you get some focused counseling to deal with the earlier pain in your life so that you can resolve it more completely. For some people, doing this exercise can stir up a lot of painful feelings, even days or weeks later. If you find this happening to you, you may want to consider going for some counseling to help support you in working through your issues.

If you feel up to doing this exploration on your own, it is important to be sure you have at least one supportive person you can share your feelings with. Consider who that person will be and talk with him or her about what you are doing. Ask if he or she would be willing to have you share a writing exercise you will be doing related to trying to better understand the source of your fear of public speaking or performing. This person does not need to do anything but listen and talk to you in a supportive and caring way. He or she should not try to analyze your situation or solve your problems. The support person just needs to be there to hear *your story* and support you in your attempts to get beyond the pain of your past so you do not have to carry this emotional baggage around anymore.

**Getting Beyond The Pain Of The Past**

In starting this exercise, you will want to create a time and space for yourself where you will not be disturbed by others or have pressing things you have to do. You may want to set aside thirty minutes to an hour, though you may not need that much time. If you find you need more time, you may want to continue beyond an hour or set aside another time to complete the exercise. You may want complete quiet or you may want some soft music that creates an atmosphere of reflection. Be sure others know not to disturb you, and be sure that you don't wander off to answer the phone or attend to other distractions. Many of us are very uncomfortable sitting with ourselves and doing this type of inner reflection and it is tempting to create or respond to distractions in our environment. Stop yourself from doing that so you can concentrate fully on this exercise. Be sure you have paper and pen to write with and find a comfortable place to write.

Read through all instructions before you start this writing exercise. Start by closing your eyes and doing some deep breathing to relax your mind and body. Begin to think back to your earlier life history, going back as far as you can remember. Think back to times when you might have felt:

- Afraid, unsafe, or trapped in a situation you could not get out of
- Disapproved of, not accepted, or inadequate in some way

- Harshly criticized or put down
- Helpless, powerless, or felt a loss of control over what was going on around you
- Embarrassed, ashamed, or not good enough
- Different and that you didn't belong
- That you could never do enough or be enough to please others and that you were a disappointment to others

Reflect also on your recent past and current life circumstances, thinking about the stresses and pressures you are experiencing at this stage in your life. Once you feel some connection with your life experience, past and present, open your eyes and start writing. Don't worry about organization, grammar, or punctuation in your writing. Your writing should reflect a free association to your life experience and your feelings about how that experience has affected you. You might write about one particular situation or event or many different things. Don't worry about being right or wrong in this exploration. Trust your instincts to lead you in the right direction. Try to connect with any powerful emotions that trigger in doing this exercise. Rather than do this exercise in a detached, intellectual manner, allow yourself to connect emotionally and compassionately with your inner pain and struggle, as that is where the greatest healing potential lies. Remember, if you are not emotionally ready to do this work on your own, do not start this exercise and consult with a professional instead.

Once you begin writing, you might find yourself confused or unsure if you are getting to the source of the problem. Just trust your gut instincts and continue to write. Be sure you have some tissue available as you may find yourself tearful as you feel the pain of the experiences you are writing about. If you do feel tearful, try not to hold back the tears as you may have in the past. It is healing to be with your true feelings and allow full expression to these feelings.

Remember, we are not out to point the finger and blame

our parents or anyone else for our problems. We are simply trying to understand and connect with the deeper part of ourselves that holds the source of our fear and shame. It is in this deeper connection with ourselves that we have the greatest possibility for healing from the pain that has given rise to our fear of public speaking or performing. This is certainly true of my own experience. As I put words to the experience of pain from my own past and connected with the tremendous loss of control that I felt back then, I was able to free myself up to be more connected to my present as an adult. I was able to let go of the feelings of helplessness and powerlessness that the frightened child I once was had experienced.

When you have completed your writing exercise, make a time to share your writing with your support person as soon as possible while it is still very fresh in your mind. Explain to this person that you simply want them to listen first without interrupting, and then respond in any caring and supportive way that comes naturally to them. It is important to choose someone who is not emotionally involved in what you are writing about as you need them to be attentive to your feelings and perceptions and not caught up with their own. It is also important to choose someone who you believe has the capacity to be compassionate and supportive in their response to you. After you read your writing to this person, share any additional feelings and thoughts with them before they respond to you. Share with them what type of beliefs and meaning you created about yourself, others, and your world based on your experience. Share with them how you think your response to these life experiences may have created the source of your current fear of public speaking or performing. Share with them a possible set of new beliefs and meaning that you can create that can free you from whatever inner struggle and turmoil you have experienced. After you fully discuss this with your support person, I encourage you to rip up your writing as a symbolic gesture of letting go of the past and clearing a fresh new

space to create your present and future. If you don't want to
rip it up, then store it somewhere out of reach so it is not part
of your present living space. At a later time you may want to
dispose of it as you recognize you no longer need to hold onto
pain from your past. The message to yourself is that the past is
over and you now can create a present and future of your own
choosing, not dictated by past circumstances.

This exercise certainly takes a lot of courage, as most of us
do anything we can to avoid feeling emotional pain or discomfort. While this exercise is not essential to managing or reducing your fear of public speaking or performing, I highly recommend it for those of you who want to go the extra length to
uncover the source of your fear and work to heal the earlier
pain you may be holding. The writing exercise alone may just
be the start of this process, and you may want to consider some
further writing, reading, or counseling to more fully resolve
your feelings about your earlier pain. Resolving this pain happens when you can:

- Identify the painful experiences in your life;
- Be with that pain in a nurturing and supportive way;
- Share that pain with someone you can trust;
- Understand the meaning and beliefs you have created
  about yourself, others, and your world;
- Detach from that pain and work toward creating a new,
  more resourceful meaning and interpretation from the per-
  spective of your adult-self.

Through this process, you are able to make conscious what
is driving your fear on a deeper level and have more control
over the meaning you attach to the circumstances of your life.

Most people in my classes have gotten a lot out of this writing exercise as they come to understand and share the connection between past pain and their current fear of public speaking or performing. On occasion, someone is not able to come
up with much that they have felt pain over in the past, and they

may feel frustrated by this exercise. If this happens for you, don't despair! Just accept that this is happening and stay open to anything that may occur to you along the way regarding any connection to your earlier or recent history. Perhaps you did not experience something as particularly painful, but instead felt frustrated, overwhelmed, or confused at times, which led you to lose faith and belief in yourself. If you cannot come up with anything, do not force it. Instead, you may want to consider revisiting this chapter and trying this exercise again in the future.

**SUMMARY:**

- Our earlier, painful life experience can get projected onto our present experience with public speaking or performing, creating similar feelings to those we experienced at an earlier time in our lives.
- This process is usually unconscious and we are often unaware of the connection between our past pain and our current struggle with public speaking or performing.
- It is helpful to better understand the source of our deep fear and mistrust so we can resolve the issues from our past and no longer project them onto our present experience.
- It is helpful to share *your story* with a supportive person who you can trust. It is important that you do not attempt this inner work on your own if you feel overwhelmed by it. It is recommended that you pursue some counseling if this is the case, or if you want to do some deeper work to further your understanding and healing from earlier pain in your life.
- If your fear has surfaced more recently, it is helpful to reflect on the stresses and pressures in your recent past that may have triggered this fear. It is also helpful to do the writing exercise and explore any earlier life circumstances that may have led you to be vulnerable to developing this

type of fear.

**ACTION STEPS:**

- Do the writing exercise described in this chapter if you feel ready for an inner exploration of the source of your pain associated with public speaking or performing. After sharing your story with a supportive person, discuss where the connections may be in what you have experienced in your life, and what you project onto the public speaking or performing situation. Consider a new, more resourceful interpretation and meaning for your life challenges, based on your adult perspective and understanding.

- Choose a quiet time and place of your own. Close your eyes and go back to painful or uncomfortable memories in your past, or recent inner conflict you may have experienced. Now create a new story of your own making, where *you* are in control. In your mental imagery, create a new memory of your history where you have the power and control over what is happening, rather than feeling helpless and vulnerable. Or, create a new image of your recent stresses and pressures and see yourself handling whatever has to be handled in an effective and confident way. Seek out professional help if you feel overwhelmed by this exercise or if you want to pursue this work further.

## Chapter 10

### *Overcoming Self-Consciousness And Inhibition*

I often felt like an awkward and self-conscious teenager whenever I had to get up and speak in front of others. The teenage years are often characterized as years of feeling unsure of ourselves and having a lot of self-doubt. There is typically an extraordinary focus on what other people think of us, especially our peers, and a fear that we will not be liked and accepted. There is usually a deep concern about rejection and an uncertainty about who we really are. We often feel like we are different and do not belong. There is also tremendous self-focusing, where we feel that the world revolves around us. As teenagers, we are so concerned with how we look to others that we rarely, if ever, concern ourselves with the feelings and needs of others.

Now, as adults, it is time to grow beyond this self-focused, self-conscious state where we are afraid to be seen and heard by others. The fear of visibility, or being the center of attention, is one of the deepest fears we hold about public speaking or performing. There is a fear that people can see right through us and see all of our fears and perceived inadequacies. We hold shame about ourselves for having any weaknesses, and we are afraid that people will discover the deeper vulnerability that resides within us. We do not trust people enough to feel we can show our vulnerability. There is a fear that people will not accept us, and they may even take advantage of us. Our guard is up and we do not want people to see us too closely. We are afraid that we cannot control what people see about us when we are on display in front of an audience.

We tend to be very afraid of loss of control and generally try to control ourselves and situations around us. We become afraid that we will not be able to control ourselves or others when we are in a situation of public speaking or performing. The more we anxiously try to take control, the more we fear the loss of control, which further fuels feelings of helplessness and panic. This terrifies us because we do not trust that we will be safe and come out of the situation okay if we do not have control. It becomes a vicious cycle - our strong need to have control fuels our deep fear of loss of control.

When we are in this fearful state, we are very constricted and inhibited in our presentation of ourselves. We become very fearful of making a mistake or doing something wrong. It is as though we feel we are walking a tightrope suspended high in the air without any protection or support. If we make one wrong step, we may plunge to our death. We are very afraid of exposing our true selves and feel we have to be someone we are not.

One of my biggest fears was the fear of being seen as inappropriate. It was important to me to always look and act very mature, professional, and together. I deeply feared loss of respect and credibility if I behaved in a manner that was unacceptable to others. I became very constricted and inhibited in the way I presented myself, believing I had to be a certain way to gain the acceptance and approval of others. The thought that my fear might be seen by others terrified me. All of my energy was going into trying to appear calm and controlled. I so desperately tried to look good so that others would accept me and approve of me. Wow! What a wasted use of precious life energy!

### Stepping Out Of The Comfort Zone

Some of the biggest breakthroughs for me have come when I have been able to step outside of my comfort zone and allow myself to do something seemingly inappropriate and out of the ordinary. One thing that helped me immensely in overcoming my fear of visibility in front of a group was an exercise I did in a personal development workshop that I attended a few years ago. As part of the exercise, I stood in front of a large group and allowed the group to fully see me without any exchange of words. As I first looked out on the group of about eighty people I felt terrified. I felt very tense, awkward, and self-conscious. As I continued with this exercise, I moved beyond my self-consciousness and started to see a dramatic shift in my perception of myself and others. I started to feel the love, acceptance, and caring of the group; and I started to connect with people in a more genuine and authentic way than I had ever before experienced. After a few minutes, I was overcome by emotion and started to sob in front of the group. Rather than feeling embarrassed, I felt the healing of a lot of pain in that moment. I realized I had tried to stay hidden for so many years, not trusting that others would accept me if they saw my vulnerability. Now I was coming out of hiding and I was safe! I felt accepted and supported by others, and I felt like I belonged.

Through this exercise I was able to free myself of my over-concern about being accepted and approved of by others. I had come to believe that I had to constantly prove myself to be accepted and to feel as though I had the right to be in front of others. I began to shift my perception about myself and about how others view me. Instead of feeling I had to work so hard to earn the acceptance of others, I started to trust that I am an acceptable person, that I do belong, and that I have the right to be in front of others. I began to feel safe in being who I really am and not feel that I have to keep proving myself. As I felt safer in being in front of others, I no longer felt such a need to be in control, nor did I fear that I would lose control. I felt I could be more genuine and real, and I started to see the audience as more genuine and real. I also began to accept the caring and support that the audience had to offer me.

In my class, we do a visibility exercise with the focus on creating a deeper connection with members of the group through eye contact without words. It is a very powerful exercise. At first, there is a feeling of dread in the room when I describe what we will be doing. There is an awkwardness and discomfort in doing this exercise for most people. While this is true, many people have told me that it was one of the most powerful exercises in breaking down the barrier between themselves and others and reducing the fear of being visible in front of a group.

Once you start to connect with people on a more real and genuine level and feel the support and acceptance from others, you begin to feel safe. This is not to say that all audiences have a supportive and accepting manner. Whenever I am in front of an audience that is not so supportive, I tune in more to any positive energy there may be in the room, and I focus on creating that energy whenever possible. Instead of feeling threatened by an unsupportive audience, I now see the possibility of trying to understand where the negativity is coming from and helping my audience to reduce its defensive posture and shift more into an open and receptive posture. Now that I feel a more unconditional acceptance of myself, I am not striving to gain acceptance from my audience. I am more concerned that my audience is in a positive and receptive state so they will get the most out of the experience. I want them to walk away from the experience feeling they have gotten value and that it has made a difference in their lives.

**The Risk Of Appearing Foolish**

Another major breakthrough for me was allowing myself to risk appearing inappropriate and foolish in front of a group. I have now come to redefine the meaning of this. Instead of being so afraid of losing respect and looking foolish if I did something out of the ordinary, I have come to realize that doing something novel and unpredictable can actually add new interest and energy to the group. Reducing my own inhibitions and being a bit playful with the audience can allow the audience to reduce its inhibitions and to relate to me more as a real person. It can actually increase my connection with the group and level the playing field, so the group can relate to me better. It can also create laughter and fun in the group, which can break down barriers and add more group cohesion.

I remember trying this out for the first time with a business group I spoke to on the topic of Stress Management. It was a formal business meeting, and I was trying to think of a way to do something a little unpredictable and playful, within reasonable bounds for this environment. I came up with something that was outside of my usual definition of appropriateness which made me slightly uncomfortable, but I did it anyway for the purpose of being more playful and more real with my audience. Part way through my talk, I shared one of my favorite ways to manage my stress. I pulled out a picture of my beloved golden retriever Celia and as I passed the picture around, I described the comfort and calm I experience with my dog. I shared with the group that I bring my dog to work, which has a tremendous effect on reducing stress in my office environment. In the past I would have been very hesitant to reveal anything so personal with the group, and I would have judged it to be totally inappropriate to show a picture of my dog to a business group I was addressing. This time I did not mind if I was seen as inappropriate because my purpose was to create a more real connection with the group and to create some fun and playful energy at the outset. When

I did this, I noticed very blank and distant faces start to soften and light up, with smiles coming to people's faces. It worked! I had made a human connection with these people, and after that they seemed even more responsive and interested in hearing what I had to say.

### Reducing Inhibition

In my class I ask participants to do an exercise to reduce inhibition and to create a light and playful energy with the group. I've called it *the outrageousness exercise*, where participants are asked to do something in front of the group that is out of character for them and makes them feel foolish. Class members usually consider this exercise and *the visibility exercise* to be two of the hardest, yet most helpful, exercises. These two exercises pull us way outside of our comfort zones and quickly begin to break down barriers of inhibition and self-consciousness. The outrageousness exercise allows us to risk appearing foolish and know that it does not matter. What matters most is that we can be energetic, unpredictable, playful, fun, and entertaining to our audience. It wakes up our audience and creates lively interest and energy in the room. This is a very different use of ourselves than when we are tense, uptight, overly serious, and even glum, trying not to make a mistake or look like a fool. When we begin to break down our barriers, and step outside of the box of our stereotypical way of behaving in front of an audience, it is extremely liberating. One participant referred to it as being "like a caged bird set free."

I am not suggesting that we go into every speaking or performance event ready to do something foolish or inappropriate. What I am suggesting is that we give ourselves permission to express ourselves more spontaneously and creatively without being so caught up with the fear of looking foolish. I am also suggesting that we consider ways with which we can energize ourselves and our audience by doing things that are spontaneous, playful, and fun.

**SUMMARY:**

- We can often feel like an awkward and self-conscious teenager when we are presenting ourselves in front of a group, fearing we will not be liked or accepted by others.

- Fear of visibility is one of the deepest fears we hold. We are afraid people will be able to see through us and see all of our fears and perceived inadequacies. We do not trust others enough to allow them to see our vulnerability.

- Our strong need to have control over ourselves and our situation fuels our deep feelings of loss of control. The more we anxiously try to get control, the more we fear the loss of control, which fuels feelings of helplessness and panic.

- When we are in this fearful state, we become very constricted and inhibited. We try to be someone we are not. We need to feel safe being who we really are in front of others and not feel we have to prove ourselves as acceptable and worthy.

- Our biggest breakthroughs come when we can be real and genuine in front of others and relate to the realness and genuineness of others.

- It is incredibly liberating to give ourselves permission to risk looking foolish or inappropriate in front of others. It gives expression to our creative energy and allows us to be spontaneous, playful, and fun-loving. It also gives the audience permission to let down its barriers and participate more openly and freely.

**ACTION STEPS:**

- It may be tempting to skip over the exercises in this section. If you are feeling this way, be sure to reconnect with your earlier commitment to do whatever it takes to overcome this fear. While these two exercises will likely make you feel very uncomfortable, they also have the potential to bring the greatest rewards in terms of reducing your self-consciousness and inhibition.

### The Visibility Exercise

Gather together a group of five or more people. These can be friends, family, coworkers, neighbors, or anyone else. Pets don't count!

Arrange the people so they are sitting in front of you and you are standing in front of them, with enough distance so you can see everyone and everyone can see you. Tell them you are working on reducing your fear of being the center of attention and your fear of looking foolish.

Let them know you will be having only eye contact with them in this exercise and neither you nor the group should talk. Give gentle, focused eye contact with each person until you feel deeply connected with each of them and their humanness. When you look at each person, connect with what you like and love about him or her. Connect with each person's uniqueness as he or she connects with yours. Allow yourself to be vulnerable and to receive love and support from each individual. Likewise, connect with the deeper human vulnerability of each person and give love and support to each one. Feel a healing energy pass between you and each person in the group.

Give each person sufficient eye connect so that you have gotten beyond the initial awkwardness and are now relating to each person on a deeper, more genuine level. Talk to yourself in resourceful ways when you feel awkward so you support yourself through those moments. Create a body language that supports openness and receptivity to others.

Don't rush through this exercise! Go back again if you feel incomplete in relating to any given individual, or the group as a whole, and do some more until you feel more at ease with the connection you are making with others.

After you are finished with this exercise, let the group know what you have just experienced and thank them for providing a safe environment for you to do this exercise. Also give them an opportunity to share with you their experience of you in this exercise and what it felt like for them to participate.

As if this weren't challenging enough, the next exercise will likely stretch you even further outside of your comfort zone. Remember, the more uncomfortable the exercise, the more potential for breaking down barriers!

**The Outrageousness Exercise**

What we usually do in class is have the person in front of the group do something silly and out of character for him or her. I offer the option of dancing in front of the group, which many people are very reluctant to do because they would feel foolish and self-conscious. Or, they can choose something else that will make them feel silly and foolish, such as singing a song or acting out some funny routine.

While most of my class participants are very timid about doing this initially, they wind up having fun as they create a joyful, playful energy in the room. The group ends up roaring in laughter with this exercise as everyone seems to benefit from breaking down barriers of inhibition and rigidity. I play outrageous dance music and ask people to be as silly and playful as possible.

Allow yourself to do the same in front of your group. If you choose to dance, play some great dance music that will allow you to let go. Be prepared with the music and a tape or CD player. Make sure you have adequate space to move around, whatever you choose to do. Watch people watching you and be playful with your audience. Be sure to give eye contact to the group members as you behave foolishly. Delight in their smiles and laughter. Allow yourself to experience laughter and joy as you release your inhibitions. Be free to express yourself creatively. Do not just do the same movement back and forth in a robotic way. Really let go of all of the inhibitions that have stopped you from freely expressing yourself in front of others. Risk looking foolish and know it doesn't matter!

You can be who you are and enjoy this new life energy you have freed up. After you have behaved foolishly in front of others for at least two minutes, stop and share with the group what it was like for you and thank them for providing a safe place for you to risk appearing foolish and inappropriate. Allow them an opportunity to share how they experienced you during this exercise and what it was like for them to participate.

After doing these two exercises, many class participants experience a feeling of liberation from the depth of self-consciousness and inhibition they have been holding onto for years. You may want to repeat these exercises with the same group, or with a different group of people, to further desensitize you to being the center of attention and to the fear of looking foolish.

## Chapter 11

### *Creating New Possibilities*

We are so used to feeling intense discomfort with public speaking or performing, or even just the thought of it, that it seems virtually impossible to feel any kind of joy or pleasure associated with it. What most of us hope for is that the fear will go away and we will be able to get through the experience without panic or dread. It is important that we expand our vision and know that we can have much more than that. We can actually come to enjoy the activity of public speaking or performing!

Most of us immediately think, "I'll never be able to feel like that," which then stops us from even trying to take it to the next level. I had once believed that there was no way that I could ever enjoy public speaking. I had created limitations in my self-image that did not allow me to enjoy being the center of attention or to feel worthy enough to be in a leadership position speaking to others. At some point I recognized that I was the one who was creating this barrier, and there was no reason why I could not be someone who enjoyed public speaking. What a revelation that was! I began to expand my definition of myself and saw a vision for myself as someone who could find joy in the experience of speaking in front of others. I discovered that it is possible to change your self-image and become more of the person you want to be, if you want it badly enough.

We must become aware of the habitual ways of thinking and expressing ourselves, verbally and nonverbally, that condition us to have negative associations to public speaking or performing. For example, if our typical way of responding to a speaking or performing opportunity is to tense up and think or express something like, "Oh no, I won't be able to do this...how can I get out of it?", our negative associations will continue to be reinforced. Instead, we must begin to identify with and adopt patterns of behavior of people who are not only not afraid of speaking or performing, but who also actually enjoy it!

When I have read about or spoken to people who enjoy public speaking or performing, I see some common threads. Typically, these people relate the great feeling that comes with knowing they have the ability to influence a large number of people's lives for the better. They enjoy the ability to contribute and make a difference in the lives of others. They see they can do this more effectively in a group setting because they can affect many more lives than in one-on-one interactions. Many people also enjoy the creative process of developing and delivering a presentation or performance. They value the opportunity to express themselves and be listened to. They feel a real sense of accomplishment in their efforts. Many also enjoy the leadership role that goes along with public speaking or performing. They enjoy the feeling of achievement and personal empowerment that comes with *stepping up* and meeting a challenge.

It is essential that we stop focusing on and expressing our

fear and discomfort with public speaking or performing, for the more that we express fear and discomfort, the more fear and discomfort are reinforced and conditioned. We need to develop more positive associations to speaking or performing and condition these new associations in the way we think and express ourselves. We need to expand our self-image to see a new possibility for ourselves. Instead of setting our sights on simply reducing or eliminating fear, we can raise our standards and look for the joy and fulfillment that are possible in being seen and heard.

I have done a number of things to raise my standards and open up to a broader vision of what is possible for me in the area of public speaking. One of the most important things I have done is to constantly seek to learn from people who have what I want in this area, as well as in the general area of self-empowerment. I read many books, listen to audiotapes, attend personal development seminars, and talk to people to learn directly from them. I model myself after people whom I admire and imagine myself thinking and behaving in new, expanded ways. I follow many of the principles that these people live by and I find myself creating new possibilities for myself. In doing this I do not try to be someone else, but I do work to free myself of my own self-imposed limitations and create my own best self.

Another thing I do is to hold myself accountable for my own growth and development. I will no longer accept being less than I can be. This means that I will now take more risks to stretch myself beyond my comfort zone, seeing it as an opportunity for growth. Avoidance behavior, excuses, and letting myself off the hook are no longer acceptable to me. I think of the saying, *"No guts, No glory,"* which I now live by. I look for ways to practice courage rather than hide in fear from these opportunities. I experience feelings of tremendous glory when I continue to break through limitations from my past and forge ahead with a new vision of who I am and what is possible in my life. I also look for opportunities to practice the value of contribution to others, knowing that is what our ultimate purpose in speaking or performing is all about.

One of my greatest joys is creating a learning environment in which personal transformation can take place. This is exactly what I do in my *No More Stage Fright* classes. It is an incredible experience to watch people in my classes release the hold that fear has had on them and to move toward new possibilities for increasing courage and confidence in speaking and performing.

### Revisiting Class Participants

I would now like to have the class participants with whom we visited in Chapter Three share some of their experiences and insights after they took my *No More Stage Fright* class. They share ways in which they have applied some of the principles and strategies they learned in class to help them expand their own possibilities of growing beyond their fear.

### Steven C.

Steven said, "Attending the class gave me insight into the fact that many people from all walks of life have faced this problem. I was encouraged by this and no longer feel weak or defective. Knowing that I am not alone immediately helped me to feel better about myself."

Steven reported, "The greatest benefit for me was the visibility exercise because I was able to stand in front of a group and look directly at people. This helped me because I knew nothing was expected of me so I could just stand there and look at this beast that I had been so scared of. It was far and away the most liberating experience I have ever had related to public speaking. The crazy dancing afterward was also part of the liberation process. Normally I would have been mortified to dance in front of a group, which I did in the outrageousness exercise, but it was actually fun. I think a huge barrier started to crumble for me at that moment."

Steven says there are many things from the class he is trying to practice. "I have tried to cut back on or eliminate caffeine from my diet, and I have tried to improve my diet in general. I also frequently practice the relaxation techniques, including visualization of "a safe, special place." I listen to relaxing music while doing relaxation exercises. I also view my videotape to see that I wasn't really as bad as I thought. The class gave me a sense of hope that I haven't had in years. Getting up in front of the group was a big step for me and I plan to stick to my Action Plan, which includes joining a speaking group in my area for further practice of what I have learned."

Another key thing for Steven is understanding that there will probably always be some level of fear, but as "I work on the fear it will become manageable so that it won't prevent me from accepting any speaking engagements that I may have. All in all, the class put me into a positive mind-set where I finally believe I can overcome my fear." He says the most important thing for him is accepting the fear and learning to deal with it. He realizes there is no single quick fix that will completely eliminate the problem. The main thing he is focused on is to stay positive and to keep working at it. "It is going to be a jour ney for me but I just have to keep at it, to keep challenging myself to go a little farther than I have gone before."

**Julie R.**

Julie says she now has "a mental tool kit" that she uses to deal with the problem. She says that accepting her panic and understanding that it "won't kill me" was the first thing. "I now believe that letting my panic stop me from sharing information is selfish, as it does not allow me to make a contribution to others." Julie also remembers, *"It's not about me,* it's about the subject I am speaking on." And she even tries to have fun now while speaking! She rereads her notes from class before every presentation and keeps "a cheat sheet" of reminders right in front of her. She says that kava kava, an herbal remedy, has also really helped her keep the panic manageable.

"Of all the classes I have taken in my life, this has had the most profound effect. Coming from an instructor who has been there, and has cured herself, has made us all realize we could get there too."

## Austin P.

Austin says that he still has some of the thoughts and images that he had before, but that the techniques discussed have helped him reduce the intensity of his fear. "I recently performed several times in front of a large group and I experienced less fear than I have in the past." He uses many of the techniques everyday, and before a presentation he often reviews his notes from the class to remind him to take the focus off himself.

Austin says that taking the class was "one of the best things I have ever done." He says that being in a safe environment with other people with the same fears "took away much of my shame." He now realizes that his fear is common and that it can actually be controlled or eliminated. "The only way anyone can ever eliminate or reduce their fears is to confront them. In fact, I learned to welcome the times when I am uncomfortable because this is the only way for me to grow as a person." He says he uses many of the techniques he learned, including deep breathing, accepting his fear, focusing on reality, and listening to his *inner parent*. "I am thankful to get out of my comfort zone and to be able to confront my fears head on. I feel much more in control of my life now."

## Isabel M.

Isabel has applied some of the principles and strategies of the class but admits she needs to work on others. The ones she has worked on are the breathing and replacing negative self talk with positive thoughts. In general, she tries to envision personal success around any number of potential speaking opportunities and finds that this creates "a better picture for how it could be. This has been helpful to me because it reinforces the positive feedback I get from others instead of discounting that feedback." She used to create a lot of negative energy "that doesn't do me any good." She is starting to see herself in the positive way that others seem to see her which, she says, is "a major breakthrough for me! While it is important for me to get beyond this, I now realize it isn't the most important issue in my life, and I don't need to feel as if I am a failure because of it."

Isabel says that the most important thing she has learned is that the only limitations for her are the ones that she sets for herself. Hiding from the fear has been worse for her than facing it head on. "Taking control of this fear and making a commitment to overcome it has already provided enormous relief." She is starting to see herself as somebody who not only can deliver a presentation, but who can also do a pretty good job at it as well!

**Jim B.**

Jim says that the class confirmed some beliefs and provided new information in two important areas: coping techniques and the opportunity to begin to change how he perceives himself. "The techniques that work best for me include good preparation through proper exercise, diet, and rest, not rehearsing every word ad nauseam, and envisioning my safe place." Although the techniques are helpful, the opportunity to change his self-perception has been the most valuable for him. The videotape of his talks during class, combined with written feedback from classmates, has provided surprising insights into how others react to him and how he sees himself. "When I viewed the video for the first time, I was amazed to see that much of my anxiety did not show! I didn't look or sound as bad as I expected to." The written feedback from classmates indicated that he appeared confident. He had not expected that and found it great to see that sort of comment from several people. He also benefited from some constructive criticism. He learned he needed to project more energy and smile more. "Getting that feedback made a lot of sense and using those suggestions has helped me to further reduce my anxiety."

Jim says, "We shouldn't assume we fully understand our speaking problem on our own. I feel we need to share our fears with others, try some exercises, and get some feedback. One's self-perception isn't necessarily accurate and you may be pleasantly surprised by the feedback you get from others!"

**Kathryn M.**

Realizing the source of the fear has been a big help for Kathryn, as well as learning to be aware of all of the negative messages we tell ourselves. "What especially helped me was the technique of taking the focus off of ourselves, to be less self-conscious, and learning that when we are speaking it is not about us. Instead, it is about the message we have to give and that we have the right to communicate." She learned we can all make a difference and we owe it to others to do so. Since taking the class, Kathryn says she has become "more fearless." She recently organized and led a women's retreat. "I have just come to the realization that I'm not an introvert after all, but I am an extrovert!"

**Reggie D.**

Reggie says that after the class he has tried to take a few of the principles which seemed most effective and use them in his daily life. He tries to avoid caffeine as much as possible. He also uses deep breathing a lot and is trying to use more positive visualization lately. "Since the class I have had more positive experiences than bad ones." He has had three successful interviews for a new position within his company. "The techniques I used allowed me to appear more comfortable and talk more easily in front of the interviewers." He also had a stress-free introduction and did a presentation in front of his MBA class. He says these all went very well and he was excited. "Shortly thereafter, I had to introduce myself in a training class and had some serious anxiety come back." He says he knows this will take time and he plans to continue to work on making progress. "Actually, in some odd way, I am looking forward to putting myself in these situations to get more experience and hopefully feel more comfortable." He says that the impact of the class and the techniques learned "have gone a long way in helping me make some progress in the area of public speaking."

The most important thing Reggie would like to share is, "I have made progress when I wasn't sure if there would ever be progress. It didn't happen overnight, but I have had small successes which have made me more motivated to overcome my anxiety." He speaks of the class as a great atmosphere to begin working on this type of fear and discomfort. He found it to be a very supportive atmosphere, while still challenging class participants to "get out and go for it. It really helped me to put things in perspective." He says the class was a truly diverse, friendly, and supportive group of individuals from all walks of life. "It was great!"

**Suzanne G.**

Suzanne has now made a commitment to learn how to trust herself and her own words. The course was one step in learning to do this. "For me, it has been very important to see public speaking in a practical way." She does not have the type of personality that likes "to talk for the sake of talking. I have to feel that what I am saying is important and of value to someone." The primary thing for her is to focus on the importance of what she is saying, not on her fear. "These days when

I have something to say that is important, I say it. I try to keep my fear out of the equation and just focus on what I am there to say."

## Michael D.

Michael says he still experiences the symptoms, but, "The big difference is that now I know I can speak in public and that it really isn't so bad." Since taking the class, his fear has lessened and his symptoms are less severe. This has allowed him to substantially reduce the dosage of Inderal he takes. "I have found hope in a seemingly hopeless situation, knowing it is possible to overcome my problem." He says it takes courage, and perhaps anger, to wish "to attack and cure the problem." He feels the medication has been "a savior to me and that taking the class was one of the bravest things I have ever done." He thinks it is important for those who have this problem early in life to have it addressed at that point and to practice public speaking at a young age so that the phobia does not become ingrained.

## Diana A.

Diana says that the affirmations "I have a right to express myself" and "I can hear constructive criticism" have been extremely helpful to her. Also, the affirmation, "I do not serve the world by playing small" has been the greatest inspiration to her. Understanding what a phobia is and how the brain and body send messages to each other that lead to a spiraling effect of fear has helped a great deal as well. "My experience of being in the class and learning to do the deep breathing and grounding myself in reality was very helpful. The other thing that was most helpful was writing out the story of the source of my fear and throwing it away." This gave her a place to say, "From this moment on, I make a fresh start." She also follows the advice of her singing teacher, who told her to say a thank-you prayer for her gift each time before she goes on stage. Diana says,

"You are never too old to turn out to be who you really are."

**Tuzines N.**

Tuzines says she has held on to the benefits she got from the class. "I play my violin with more ease and with a lot less nervousness. I practice techniques I learned from the class before a performance or speech. I also take deep breaths and reassure myself that I will do fine." She prepares herself through practice beforehand and treats her concerts as practices to ease some of the pressure. "The shaking in my hands is greatly reduced, resulting in a smoother, better performance." She thinks the things she learned from the class are great and that the methods have lasting value.

Again, I want to express my deepest appreciation to those class participants who shared their experiences in this book. I also want to acknowledge all of my class participants for their courage and determination to face their fears and not continue to be limited by them.

My mission is to create and inspire courage, personal power, and positive energy in others. It is my hope that I have achieved my purpose in writing this book. I thank you for the opportunity to make a difference in your life. I feel a kindred spirit with you in having suffered from a similar life challenge. I want for you all that I have found for myself, which is to break through your self-imposed limitations and become more than you ever dreamed possible. I hope my story can inspire you to raise the standards by which you live your life and to no longer accept the limitations of fear and self-doubt. My hope is that you break through these limitations so we can all benefit from whatever gifts you have to contribute to our world.

**SUMMARY:**
• We are so used to feeling fear and discomfort associated with public speaking or performing that we create limita-

tions in our self-image, thinking we could never be someone who enjoys speaking or performing in front of others.

- We need to stop focusing on and expressing our fear and
discomfort as this continues to reinforce and condition
these feelings. Instead, we need to create and reinforce
new, more positive associations with public speaking and
performing.

- We can do this by learning from others who enjoy the
process of speaking or performing in front of others. We
can learn what it is these people think and do that allows
them to experience pleasure in speaking or performing and
model ourselves after them in these ways.

- We can expand our self-image and vision of ourselves and
create new possibilities for self-expression we never
dreamed possible. This takes a commitment to hold yourself to a higher standard and to risk going beyond your
comfort zone to experience the rewards on the other side.

## ACTION STEPS:

- In your journal write down a list of new associations to
public speaking or performing. Focus on the potential
pleasure and enjoyment you can experience in speaking or
performing once the fear is no longer blocking the positive
feelings. If you are having a hard time considering this just
yet, then write down the things that you would imagine
some other people find pleasurable about public speaking
or performing.

- Write a vision statement that allows you to create a new
identity of who you are as a speaker or performer. Allow
this statement to expand your self-image beyond where
you are now and guide you on your journey of becoming
who you want to be. Allow the statement to reflect a vision
of what is possible for your future, with continued commitment on your part to put in the efforts necessary to
bring this vision into reality.

- Read your vision statement twice daily for the next three months and create a mental picture in your mind of this vision manifesting itself in reality. It is most helpful if you do this at night right before going to bed so that your unconscious mind can go to work on bringing it about. It is also helpful to do it early in the morning before the distractions of the day begin.

- Plan to speak or perform in front of the group of five or more people that you brought together for the prior two exercises. Focus on the joy of self-expression and your new vision of who you want to be as a speaker or performer. Plan to speak for at least fifteen minutes and continue to add to that over time, requesting that the group come together to support you until you feel more confident as a speaker or performer. You may also want to take turns supporting other people in the group who want to gain confidence in speaking or performing and create a support group for all. Also remember to use methods learned in earlier chapters and be sure to update your Strategies List, as well as your *Success Formula* with all that you have learned thus far. Continue to review this material regularly and add to it as you discover new ways to empower yourself as a speaker or performer.

- Write down a Plan of Action to keep your progress moving forward. Things you may want to consider include more reading on the subject of speaking or performing and peak performance, looking for role models to identify with, taking my *No More Stage Fright* class, joining a group to get more practice in speaking or performing, and following through with practicing the exercises described in earlier chapters to reinforce and condition new ways of thinking and new behaviors.

## AFTERWARD

I thank you, the reader, for the opportunity to make a difference in your life. I am grateful that my own suffering has
been transformed into a mission that serves the greater good
by helping others who also struggle with this problem. I
would appreciate any feedback you have about my book and
suggestions you have for furthering my work in helping people with this fear. I welcome you to visit my web site at
www.performanceanxiety.com and complete the online survey
about your own experiences with stage fright and share any of
your reactions to reading my book. You may also email me
directly at *jesposito@performanceanxiety.com* with comments,
questions, or suggestions or call me with your feedback. I welcome your feedback as it gives me a better understanding of
how I can forward my mission. I would also appreciate it if
you would let others who need help in this area know about
my work.

For those who want further help in overcoming this fear,
you may want to consider taking my *No More Stage Fright*
weekend workshop. People have found my workshop to be
extremely helpful, as it provides a safe and supportive environment to work on overcoming your fear of public speaking
and performing. It has been especially helpful to class participants to be doing this work with other people who share this
fear and understand what you are going through. Many participants have said that being in this positive group environment has helped them to release the embarrassment and shame
about having this problem and to experience renewed faith
and optimism that they can overcome the limitations of this
fear. There are many testimonials of former class participants
on my web site, and I have included some of them in Appendix
I for your review.

I also offer a One-Day Refresher Class for people who have
taken my workshop and/or who have read my book and are
looking for a way to practice and reinforce the methods that I
teach. Please know that my overriding goal in all of my work-

shops and classes is to create a safe and supportive group environment for all and no one is ever forced or pressured to do anything they do not feel capable of doing (though everyone is supported and encouraged to do the most they are capable of doing).

In addition to my workshops and classes, I am also available for individual consultations and coaching by phone, in person, or by email. People have found consultations and coaching to be very helpful in getting individualized attention to address their specific needs and concerns and to support their ongoing progress. Additionally, I am available for consultations to businesses and can provide on-site workshops in companies.

Please check my web site from time to time to stay informed of other products and services I am developing and be sure to get on our email list if you want to receive my monthly online newsletters and occasional announcements of what I am offering. I am happy to announce that I have completed a CD as a supplement to this book, entitled *In The SpotLight – Guided Exercises to Create a Calm and Confident State of Mind, Body, & Spirit While Speaking or Performing*. Please see my web site for further information on the CD and to place an order.

Once again, I thank you for joining me on this journey. I wish you ever-increasing courage, confidence, power, and belief in yourself in your future speaking and performing experiences!

With Appreciation and Respect,
Janet E. Esposito, M.S.W.
P.O. Box 494
Bridgewater, CT. 06752
Phone: 877.814.7705 (toll free), 860.210.1499 (local)
Email: *jesposito@performanceanxiety.com*
Web site: *www.performanceanxiety.com*

## APPENDIX

### Feedback from *No More Stage Fright* Class Participants

The class changed my life! The "No More Stage Fright" class I
attended was a turning point to help me get over my terror of
public speaking.  I had been suffering from anxiety over
public speaking for over 15 years and I felt hopeless.  When I
returned from the workshop I had several presentations.  I
was skeptical at first, but I immediately applied what I had
learned and was able to give the presentations with only min-
imum anxiety.  The "No More Stage Fright" class is excellent.

> J.G.
> HR Director, Health Care

These classes are the greatest gift I have ever given myself.  I
only wish I had the courage to do it sooner!  Understanding
the fear and working through it in a safe, supportive environment has had a positive impact on many areas of my life- not
only public speaking!

> D.G.
> Manager, Technology Firm

Janet's course gave me a new lease on life.  No more gnawing
at the pit of my stomach.  She suffered this problem and her
course shows the compassion and deep understanding
of one who has recovered from it.  REGISTER, TAKE THE
COURSE, and the worst skeptic will believe.  It is incredible.
Period.

> C. E.
> Pediatrician, Health Professional

If you suffer from any type of public speaking fear, you
MUST take this course.  It will change your life.  After taking
this course many new professional, as well as social opportunities were made available to me.  I am much more relaxed in
parts of my life where I never felt relaxed before.  Attending
this class was one of the best choices I have ever made.

> S.C.
> Graduate Student

I can't thank Janet enough for the confidence she has helped
me find within myself.  The course is immensely rewarding.  I
actually enjoy speaking in public now - there is nothing more
empowering than standing in front of an audience and being
recognized.

> K.S.
> Self-employed, Personal Investor

This class turned my life around. I'd always wanted to perform in musical theater, but never did, because I was too frightened to do a singing audition. Since I took this course, not only was I able to audition, but I got big parts in two musicals in the last six months. I will always be grateful to Janet Esposito for the results she has helped me achieve.

> A.G.
> Actress, Arts

Janet's class is tremendous! You will not find a more supportive environment in which to overcome your stage fright. Her insight and suggestions, along with the hands-on experience, make this class like no other class of its kind! Attending Janet's class was the best thing I have done for myself!

> E.L.
> Clinical Scientist, Pharmaceutical Firm

Janet's class provided a safe environment for me to face this fear that has interfered with my life for as long as I can remember. Through Janet's exercises, and with the support of the class, I came to finally see "the light at the end of the tunnel." Thanks, Janet, for throwing a lifeline to me when I needed it!

> J.C.
> Real Estate Broker

Although I was terrified to speak in front of the group, I pushed myself and was thrilled that I could do it. I walked out of Janet's class thinking, "I CAN", instead of "I CAN'T."

> L.T.B.
> Paralegal, Food Products

What I've gained from taking the "No More Stage Fright" course has been priceless to me. Initially, I'd feared I'd wasted my time and money because I was too fearful to even participate in the class. Despite this I learned many wonderful things just by observing others who felt like I do. And also by taking what I was taught and practicing it until I felt comfortable enough to overcome some of the fear.

> D. P.
> Elementary School Teacher, Education

The course opened my eyes to the fact that many people from all walks of life experience anxiety over public speaking and Janet provided both encouragement and a safe environment to break free of the fear.

> R.R.
> Senior V.P., Accounting/Financial Services

I have found the classes to be of tremendous benefit and have seen very tangible results in helping me to overcome my fear. In the past, the only way I could get through speaking engagements was to take medication. My symptoms were severe - but in the class, I found that I could speak comfortably without any medication. And in the real world, my need for medication has been greatly reduced - in fact, I recently made a successful impromptu mini-speech with no medication at all. This is something that just a few short months ago, (prior to the class) I never could have done!

> J.H.
> Managing Director, Trader

This class helped me to increase my confidence in speaking before a group. I look back on how I used to feel before I took the course and see a remarkable difference today.

> J.O.
> Development & Special Events
> Director, Human Services

I think the best thing about taking the course was the sense of "safety". Without this comfort level it would not have been possible for me to participate.

> P. B.
> Network Analyst, Computer

This class definitely helped me break the barriers and stop running from my fear of public speaking. In the class you really learn how to manage the "fear" and many useful techniques to become much more confident in yourself in public speaking.

> D.H.
> Chef, Food Service

I've never been afraid of confronting my fears, but Janet's course helped me confront my fears the right way. I now have solid techniques to fall back on when I get some of those negative feelings. The entire weekend was very challenging and I felt great about "Going all out".

> D. P.
> Controller, Retail

# REFERENCES

American Psychiatric Association, 1994. *Diagnostic and Statistical Manual of Mental Disorders (DSM - IV)*, Washington, DC: APA.

Beck, A., and G. Emory, 1985. *Anxiety Disorders and Phobias: A Cognitive Perspective.* New York: Basic Books.

Bourne, E., 1995. *The Anxiety & Phobia Workbook.* California: New Harbinger Publications.

Davis, M., E.R. Eshelman, and M. McKay, 1995. *The Relaxation & Stress Reduction Workbook.* California: New Harbinger Publications.

Harris, T., 1969. *I'm OK-You're OK: A Practical Guide to Transactional Analysis.* New York: Harper & Row Publishers.

Jacobson, E., 1938. *Progressive Relaxation.* Chicago: University of Chicago Press.

Maltz, M., and D. Kennedy, 1997. *The New Psycho-Cybernetics: A Mind Technology for Living Your Life Without Limits* (audiotapes). Illinois: Nightingale-Conant Corporation.

Narrow, W., D. Rae, and D. Regier, 1999. *Prevalence of Anxiety Disorders: An NIMH Epidemiology Note.* ADAA Reporter Winter 1999, 2, 24-25.

Robbins, A., 1996. *Personal Power II: The Driving Force* (audiotapes). California: Robbins Research International, Inc.

Wrightson, C. *America's Greatest Fears,* Health, Jan/Feb 1998, Vol.12 Issue 1, p.45.

# INDEX

**A**
Abandonment, fear of 29
Abdominal distress 39
Acceptance 19, 44, 55,119, 120
Acting 27
Acting classes 28
Action, plan of 65, 139; steps 5, 12, 32-33, 35, 37, 55-56, 61-62, 78-79, 102-104, 116, 123-124, 138-139
Actors, actresses 4
Affliction, lifelong 3
Agitation 95
Air, gasping for 43
Alienation 57
Aloneness 57
Anger 12, 106, 136
Anxiety 3, 9, 12, 14, 19, 21, 22, 23, 24, 25, 26, 34, 40, 41, 42, 53, 56, 62, 70, 71, 84, 98, 133, 134; anticipatory 9; performance 4, 7, 24, 27, 40, 41; surge of 1
Anxiety attack(s) 14, 17, 18
Anxiety Disorders 8, 40
Anxiety response 9, 20
Anxious 10
Apprehension 74
Arousal response 81
Assessment 64, 68, 69
Attention 2, 12, 17, 50, 58
Audiotape(s) 4, 56, 129
Audition(s) 27, 28
Autogenic Training Method, The 97-98
Avoidance 3, 13, 25 31; tactics 3
Awkwardness 120

**B**
Baggage, emotional 105
Baseline 36
Beck, Aaron 68
Behavior(s) 12, 22, 31, 82, 95, 139; avoidance 12, 20, 31, 129
Belief(s) 10, 26, 36, 61, 63, 64, 66, 68, 69, 70-72, 73, 75, 78, 86, 91, 94, 95, 101, 103, 110, 113, 114, 133
Beta blocker 40

Power 72, 95, 116
Powerlessness 43,58
Predictions 43, 44, 59, 63, 64, 66, 68, 70-72, 73, 74, 75, 78, 83, 85, 88, 89
Preoccupation 57. 60
Presentation(s) 2, 3, 14, 15, 16, 20, 21, 24, 35, 42, 43, 61, 64, 65, 69, 71, 72, 75, 76, 88, 90, 91, 94, 95, 103, 128, 132, 134
Pressure 137
Profile, self-assessment 36
Progressive Relaxation 95-97
Psychocybernetics 92
Psychotherapist 1 (see also Therapist)
Psychology 22, 94
Public Speaking 1, 7, 8, 9, 13, 14, 15, 19, 21, 22, 23, 26, 33, 39, 40, 43, 48, 60, 64, 68, 71, 74, 75, 78, 83, 86, 90, 92, 102, 103, 106, 107, 110, 111, 113, 114, 116, 117, 118, 127, 128, 129, 130, 135, 136; fear of 7, 15, 33, 36, 57, 62

R
Racial tension 27
Rage 106
Reactions, biochemical 40, 45, 81
Reality 22, 64, 66, 68, 69, 70, 75, 78, 83, 89, 132, 136, 139
Realness 59
Reasoning, emotional 67, 70
Reassurance 28, 47
Recipe for Success 104
Reinforcement 71
Rejection 9,19, 27, 28, 29, 93, 117
Relaxation 50, 51, 95, 96, 97, 99
Respect 1, 10, 43, 47, 57, 65, 68, 69, 118, 121
Response(s) 50, 100; patterned 42
Rigidity 125
Risk(s) 3, 33, 34, 75, 93, 121, 129
Role model(ing) 11, 92

S
Safe, emotionally 11
Safety 44, 47, 55, 73, 75, 78, 83, 85, 105, 106
Scrambling technique 86
Self 60
Self-acceptance 11, 13 (see also Self-evaluation)

Vocabulary 101
Voice 18, 21, 23, 72-77, 78
Vulnerability 58, 59, 108, 117-118, 119, 124

W
Water 94
Weakness(es) 9, 11, 12, 72, 117
Well-being 82
Write, writing 78, 107, 111, 112, 113, 116, 136, 138

Y
Yoga 94

Z
Zone(s), comfort 109, 119, 122, 129, 132